POLITICAL PHILOSO

POLITICAL PHILOSOPHY NOW

The Monstrous and the Dead: Burke, Marx, Fascism

Mark Neocleous

UNIVERSITY OF WALES PRESS • CARDIFF • 2005

British Library Cataloguing-in-Publication Data
A catalogue record for this book is available from the British Library.

ISBN 0-7083-1904-1 hardback
  0-7083-1903-3 paperback

Printed in Great Britain by Cromwell Press Ltd, Trowbridge, Wiltshire

For
DB, PC and KK

Contents

Acknowledgements

Parts of the argument in what follows have been tried out in various spaces and places. Thanks to the editors and anonymous reviewers of *History of Political Thought, Contemporary Political Theory*, the *Journal of Political Ideologies*, and to my co-editors at *Radical Philosophy*.

Some of the argument regarding the tensions between Marx and cultural studies on the question of the vampire was worked into a discussion of the cultural turn in political economy and presented at the workshop on *Cultural Political Economy: Economic and Political Imaginaries*, held at Lancaster University, 4 June 2004; I thank Bob Jessop and Ngai-Ling Sum for the invite and the participants for their comments. An earlier version of the critique of cultural studies was presented at the conference 'New Myths? Science Fiction, Fantasy and Horror', at Buckingham Chilterns University College, 3 May 2003. Members of the History of Political Ideas seminar in the Institute of Historical Research kindly engaged with some of the material concerning Marx and Benjamin following a paper given there in May 2004.

Thanks to Mike Levin, David Murray, David Stevens and Stuart Elden for constructively critical comments on the manuscript, and to DB, PC and KK for all the other things that matter.

Introduction

> – It takes me so long to read the 'paper,
> said to me one day a novelist hot as a firecracker,
> because I have to identify myself with everyone in it,
> including the corpses, pal.[1]

There is a scene in Bram Stoker's *Dracula* where it becomes clear that one of the main characters, Lucy Westenra, has been bitten by the vampire and is in a trance. She appears dead, but in fact is not; she is, in the terms of the novel, 'undead', and her beauty is masking the fact. The vampire-hunter Van Helsing knows that she has been prey to the vampire and that there is now no option but to kill her 'properly', in one of the ways known to destroy vampires. So he asks Lord Godalming, Lucy's fiancé: 'May I cut off the head of dead Miss Lucy?' Godalming, perhaps unsurprisingly, objects: 'Heavens and earth, no! . . . I have a duty to do in protecting her grave from outrage.' Van Helsing responds: 'My Lord Godalming, I, too, have a duty to do, a duty to others, a duty to you, a duty to the dead.'[2]

There is a political dimension to Van Helsing's comment that has often been overlooked in commentaries on *Dracula*. The political dimension has two sides. On the one hand is the suggestion that there exists a duty to the dead: that the fight against the vampire is a fight not just for the living, but also for the dead. On the other hand, there is the idea that this duty must involve challenging the power of the undead. This second dimension is based on the understanding that some entities retain the powers of the living, or develop even greater powers, after death. In this case it is the vampire, but the point is true of the monstrous in general, for one of the fundamental characteristics of monsters is said to be that they are somehow undead.[3] At first glance these might not seem especially political issues; this book aims to show that they are deeply political. The book therefore explores the political power of the monstrous and the dead.

It is sometimes said that what distinguishes man from other animals is that man is an animal that guards its dead. Traditionally, this 'guarding' has been conducted by religion. As Elias Canetti puts it, 'no-one who studies the original documents of any religion can fail to

be amazed at the power of the dead'.[4] Because of this, the dead have
fallen largely into the hands of theology. This book aims to explore
the possibility of a more political guard. It does so by considering
what happens if we retrieve the dead from theology and place them
more firmly in political hands. This is not to suggest that the book
contains any kind of political theology, however, nor is it to propose
yet another political 'turn' to a particular religion or individual
religious thinker; there has been more than enough nonsense of that
sort recently. Rather, the intention is to consider what happens when
the dead are liberated from religion and thrust into the political
limelight. It has been said that religion's control of the dead has made
death the 'litmus test of atheism'.[5] I would like to explore what
happens if we make the dead the litmus test of politics. To do so, this
book deals with the place of the dead in the work of Edmund Burke,
Karl Marx and fascism. As we shall see, there is much that separates
these writers and traditions. What unites them, however, is that they
share a common interest in the political question of our relationship
to the dead. More importantly, I aim to show that one can distinguish
political positions in terms of their understanding of the meaning and
place of the dead. In that sense, this is a book about the politics of
remembrance which aims to show that remembrance raises all sorts of
opportunities and can have very different political connotations.
Precisely *where* the dead register in the litmus test turns into a major
dividing line for the political positions explored here – a major divide,
that is, over *how* the dead are remembered politically.

The most basic political assumption concerning the dead is to view
them as part of the past and thus incorporate them into 'tradition',
especially a national tradition.[6] Such a view leads easily into the
political doctrine most closely associated with tradition, namely
conservatism. For one of conservatism's key assumptions is that, as
Burke puts it, if society is a contract then it is a contract between the
living, those yet to be born and the dead. Because conservatism has
been so closely associated with this view, remembrance has often been
conflated with a conservative traditionalism. One aim of this book,
developed through the three chapters, is to wrestle the dead out of the
arms of conservatism. But this poses an immediate problem. Relieved
from being 'merely' tradition, the dead are in danger of becoming
adopted by the other main political ideology which likes to harp on
about the past in general and the national past in particular: fascism.
As I show in Chapter 3, fascism aims to incorporate the dead into a

more general political eschatology in which the immortal nation is thought to be founded on the *resurrected* dead. Fascists therefore like to think of their struggle as taking place partly on the terrain of the dead (in both the metaphorical and the literal sense – why, after all, do fascists so enjoy desecrating graves?). In this sense, and introducing an idea to which we shall return, one might say that the dead are not safe from fascism.

To tackle this problem and suggest a possible alternative, Chapter 2 contains a set of arguments concerning the dead, developed through the work of Marx and Walter Benjamin, which consider the ways in which Marxism might not only protect the dead from fascism in a non-conservative fashion, but might also appropriate the dead for its own cause – what might be called a Marxist politics of remembrance. Theodor Adorno once commented that 'one of the basic human rights possessed by those who pick up the tab for the progress of civilization is the right to be remembered'.[7] Building on this, my argument is that a conscious horror of the destructive effects of capital on human lives, and thus a conscious appreciation of the struggles against the domination and oppression wrought by capital, creates the possibility of incorporating the dead into Marxist politics. This incorporation, which runs against one of the main thrusts of Marx's own arguments, is based on a sense of unity with the dead because we, like them, are the victims of the same conditions of domination and oppression, and share the same sense of defeat and the same disappointed hopes. I develop this position through an account of the politics of time in historical materialism and a consideration – via critical theory – of the category of redemption. In so doing I aim to contribute to the growing body of work on redemption as a historical materialist category by contrasting redemption with two alternative and fundamentally opposed categories: reconciliation, as found in conservatism, and resurrection, as found in fascism.

In the process of making this argument it will become clear that one reason we need to address these issues is because, politically speaking, the dead are never simply dead. While we may have lost the 'promis-cuity between the living and the dead'[8] that once existed in Western culture, this does not mean that the dead do not still mean something to us. A mass of anthropological and sociological research has revealed that many people still believe what conventional religions have always maintained and what fascism likes to claim: the dead remain somehow present. Mircea Eliade (who had more than a touch of the fascist about him himself), writes that 'the almost universal conviction that the dead are present . . . is highly significant. It reveals the secret hope that, in spite of all evidence to the contrary, the dead are able to partake somehow in the world of the living.'[9] The dead leave traces: not only through generations, but also in memories, dreams and unfulfilled wishes. At the same time, however, they also sometimes leave traces of fear: the living not only mourn the dead but also sometimes fear them as sources of possible harm.[10] In particular, the dead are sometimes thought to return as a threat – as the living dead. Slavoj Žižek has suggested that

> if there is a phenomenon that fully deserves to be called the 'fundamental fantasy of contemporary mass culture', it is [the] fantasy of the return of the living dead: the fantasy of a person who does not want to stay dead but returns again and again to pose a threat to the living.[11]

Rather than play up to this idea within popular culture by talking about the living dead, I prefer to use the more traditional Gothic terminology and talk about the undead. The point here, however, is that the undead never quite return as they were when (properly) alive. They often continue in some kind of deformed, threatening or unrecognizable form: they are monstrous.

Monstrosity is all the rage these days. Contemporary popular culture teems with monsters of all sorts – aliens and fiends, vampires and mutants, zombies and 'pokemons' ('pocket monsters') – and scientific developments are constantly presented in terms of their potentially 'monstrous' implications. At the same time, 'monstering' the threatening is a common motif: journalism persistently uses 'monstrous' as a label for anything and everything it fails (though usually barely tries) to understand – the paedophile, serial killer or despotic leader are perfect examples, but many more could be given. At the same time, the monstrous has also long troubled both religion and philosophy: Timothy Beal has noted that 'we can learn something about a religious tradition by getting to know its monsters', and Mark Dorrian has commented that 'the monstrous figure is the recurring nightmare which disturbs the dream of Western metaphysics'.[12] The assumption guiding this book is that, as with the dead, we can also learn something about a *political* tradition by getting to know its monsters. I am thus interested in the ways in which the monstrous becomes a form of political expression in the three major traditions in Western politics being examined here.

Joyce Carol Oates has suggested that 'Where the "human" crosses over into the "monstrous" is after all a matter of law, theology, or aesthetic taste.'[13] We might add that it is also a question of politics. Why? Because we know deep down that what is regarded as monstrous tells us more about humans than it does about the monster. As Stanley Cavell comments,

> Isn't it the case that not the human horrifies me, but the inhuman, the monstrous? Very well. But only what is human can be inhuman. Can only the human be monstrous? If something is monstrous, and we do not believe that there are monsters, then only the human is a candidate for the monstrous.[14]

Our fascination with the monstrous has a great deal to do with our very uneasy sense that such creatures are forms of ourselves – the human gone terribly wrong. The monstrous thus points to our understanding of the precariousness of human identity, the idea that human identity may be lost or invaded and that we may be, or may become, something other than we are: monsters have something to show us about our world and ourselves. In many cases, accounts of the monstrous have tended to focus on the individual monster – Grendel in *Beowulf*, Polyphemus in the *Odyssey*, the Thing, Frankenstein's monster, and so on. This has been replicated in socio-cultural analyses of why certain individuals are seen as monstrous – the paedophile, the serial killer and so on. In this book I am interested in neither such creatures nor such social constructions. Rather, I am interested in the ways in which *collective* forces have been conceived in such terms, and thus the way in which the monstrous helps raise the political question of what kind of society we are and what kind of society we want. In some cases, such as Marx's use of the vampire, the collective force is abundantly clear. In others, such as Burke's account of the revolutionary multitude, it is decidedly unclear and some serious textual work has to be done. In yet others, such as fascism, it oscillates throughout a range of enemies fascism thinks it is fighting.

In the case of Burke, I argue in Chapter 1 that the monster functions as a political tool for dealing with a nascent mass politics. While Burke had developed in the *Philosophical Enquiry into the Origin of our Ideas of the Sublime and Beautiful* a set of categories for dealing with horror and terror, the French Revolution saw him faced with a new collective entity only beginning to emerge on the historical stage – a 'mobbish' multitude which would later become the proletariat – which at that point he felt compelled to describe in Gothic terms: as monstrous. The chapter thus uses Burke's aesthetic ideology to deepen our knowledge of the Gothic tropes in Burke's writings and to broaden our conception of the way bourgeois ideology conceptualizes order and the threats to that order. In other words, I aim to show how the discourse of monstrosity functions as an ideological tool, masking the nature of the movement Burke was at pains to undermine.

Now, this might appear as though my argument reinforces the common understanding that the discourse of the monstrous is *essentially* ideological. It is well known that the language of monstrosity is very often a way of covering up a range of thoughts and/or emotions. Hobbes, who knew quite a bit about the politics of death, also knew a fair bit about monstrosity. The striking power implicit in the image of the mythical monster of the Leviathan has understandably led to the idea that this is the central idea of Hobbes's theory of the state. But as Carl Schmitt has pointed out, Hobbes liked cover-ups. The Leviathan is nothing more than a cover for the state, in the same way that the Behemoth is a cover for revolution; Leviathan and Behemoth are the monsters of state and revolution respectively.[15] Because of such cover-ups, there is a not unreasonable tendency to assume that 'the horror genre inevitably serves ideology', as Noël Carroll puts it.[16] And my argument in Chapter 3, in which I consider the ways in which fascism configures the enemy as inherently monstrous, might well be taken as further evidence of this. As I will show, one of the functions of the monstrous as a political trope is that it is crucial to the political construction of fear and insecurity – two of the most fundamental mechanisms for the constitution of order in bourgeois society.[17] Conservatism and fascism thus depend for their existence on the construction of 'monstrous' figures – revolutionaries, communists, subversives, perverts, muggers and all sorts of entities in the darkness of history – to help keep alive the kind of fears and insecurities on which domination depends.

In that sense the chapters on Burke and fascism will show that metaphors can indeed be called upon to do the dirty work of ideology, as Bram Dijkstra puts it,[18] telescoping complex ideas and historical conditions into simple imagery and thus encouraging us to see others not as persons but as something else, something inhuman; the monster-talk in question does nothing other than defend mythical 'communities' and assist in the demand for 'order'. In Chapter 2, however, I try to show how, *pace* the point about cover-ups, Marx employs one particular character from the Gothic genre, the vampire, in an explicitly anti-ideological way: to *uncover* the nature of capital. The crucial difference between Marx on the one side and Burke and fascism on the other is this: Marx employs one specific, named and carefully chosen Gothic trope and, moreover, does so in order to point to something very real about capital rather than expressing an irrational fear about some ambiguous and unnamed monster. Whereas Burke and fascism's uses of the monstrous are shot through with all sorts of ambiguities and serve to mask some fundamental social, historical and political issues – covering up rather than uncovering – Marx invokes the vampire in order to illustrate something very specific about capital. Thus as well as doing the dirty work of ideology, metaphors can be used to clarify something fundamental – something really horrific – about the social world.

The reason for choosing Burke, Marx and fascism in dealing with the monstrous and the dead is partly because of the conflicts and tensions in their accounts. It is also because all three understood the importance of imagination, language, allusion and metaphor to political writing. In the case of Burke and Marx, we have two of the most imaginative and creative writers ever – the works of both are saturated with dramatic turns, literary allusions and imaginative tropes. And while it is certainly the case that fascism has never produced a writer as original and creative as Burke or Marx, it does have a compelling sense of how important it is to play on people's imaginations. Perhaps more than any other political doctrine, fascism knows how fear can be made to permeate the psychic life of ordinary people, infiltrating our fantasy worlds, working both on and through popular fantasies, dreams and nightmares as psychic manifestations of terror. The fantasy and actuality of 'horror' or 'terror' are thus mutually entwined, and any political argument which ignores such fears, fantasies and nightmares thus risks missing a crucial dimension of the way political discourse in general, and fascist discourse in particular, functions.

It should be clear from this last comment that although this is intended to be a book aimed at contributing to our understanding of some key themes within contemporary political discourse – political philosophy *now*, as the series title has it – it is also very much a work about the political imagination. I have dealt elsewhere with the ways in which we imagine the state.[19] This book is also about imagining: how we imagine the dead, their struggles and defeats, hopes and dreams;

and how we imagine our enemies, the monstrous political 'other'. Works in and on the imagination are inherently speculative; works that also spend a fair amount of time reading between the lines of political texts doubly so. There is therefore much in this book that is speculative. There is also much that is provocative. The question is therefore less 'Is it true?' and more 'Does it work?'[20] It is an attempt to generate new thoughts, ideas and perceptions about the monstrous and the dead, and about political thinking in general. This book has been written as a means of opening up, as well as contributing to, a debate about our relation to the monstrous and the dead.

1 • Burke: The Monstrous Multitude

The work of Edmund Burke is taken by many to represent one of the first and clearest statements of conservative politics. The attack on revolutionary action and 'abstractions' such as 'reason' combined with a defence of tradition and private property has meant that his writings are widely considered to be unsurpassed in the history of conservatism. As a confirmed part of the 'canon' of political thinkers Burke's work has also been pored over for its explicit and implicit claims concerning revolution, rights, gender, sexuality, language, theatrical politics and a whole host of other issues. In this chapter I first aim to unpick a relatively unexplored dimension to Burke's thought: the monster. The possible significance of the monster in Burke's work was first hinted at by one of Burke's contemporaries, Richard Payne Knight. Noting Burke's connection between terror and the sublime he suggested the works of those who follow Burke 'teem with all sorts of terrific and horrific monsters and hobgoblins'.[1] It was an astute comment for, as I shall show, it is not just the works of Burke's followers which teem with monsters, but Burke's works too.

In a letter to his son from 1789 Burke comments on 'the portentous State of France – where the Elements which compose Human Society seem all to be dissolved, and a world of Monsters to be produced in the place of it'.[2] This seemingly throwaway comment in fact picks up on a theme which resonates throughout Burke's *Reflections on the Revolution in France* (1790). Burke refers to the new 'monster of a constitution' composed from 'a monstrous medley of all conditions, tongues, and nations'. There is also a new 'spirit of money-jobbing and speculation' which creates a 'volatilized' form of property and 'assumes an unnatural and monstrous activity'. Similarly the emerging 'military democracy' or 'municipal army' is described as 'a species of political monster'. All in all then, the new society is a 'monstrous tragi-comic scene', a 'monstrous fiction' in which 'publick measures are deformed into monsters'.[3] It also picks up on a comment Burke had made much earlier, in his *Thoughts on the Cause of the Present Discontents* (1770) about 'that monstrous evil of governing in concurrence with the opinion of the people'.[4]

On a superficial level such claims may appear fairly innocuous. It is well known that much of Burke's attack on the French revolutionaries plays on issues concerning the imagination: he comments, for example, on the importance of the 'moral imagination' which covers 'the defects of our naked shivering nature', the way 'acts of rapacious despotism present themselves to [our] imagination'.[5] As early in his intellectual career as May 1747 he opposed a particular motion at a debating club by commenting that if it were passed it 'would take away our Spirit by reducing our speeches to dry logical reasoning'.[6] The attempt to avoid dry logical reasoning permeates virtually all his writings and speeches. When the *Reflections* first appeared in 1790 Horace Walpole commented that its 'wit and satire are equally brilliant' and that its metaphors and allusions are so powerful that they are almost impossible to translate.[7] 'Chock full of feverish metaphors and gorgeous wording', Don Herzog comments, the *Reflections* 'is a deeply literary text, no more amenable to logic chopping than an epic poem or a first-rate novel.'[8] Maybe, then, Burke's references to the monstrous are nothing other than one of the many rhetorical flourishes, stylistic turns and metaphorical innovations – one of the 'poetical liberties' in the 'dramatic performance' of the *Reflections*, as Thomas Paine describes it[9] – for which Burke is rightly known and which he consciously opted to use. So if, as he suggests, 'a Government of the nature of that set up at our very door has never been seen, *or even imagined*',[10] then it may perhaps make perfect sense to allow his description of this hitherto unimaginable thing as 'monstrous' and leave it at that. But if, on the other hand, literary style has any connection with political presuppositions, then the choice of metaphor might be important. In other words, if the metaphors writers use offer clues to some of the more substantive arguments in their work then it might just be worth following through the trope of the monster in Burke's arguments.

On this basis, this chapter has a number of interrelated aims. First, I aim to show that the figure of the monster in Burke's arguments provides a further link between his work on the Revolution and his much earlier essay on the sublime and the beautiful; in this way I aim to make a relatively minor contribution to the developing body of literature on Burke's aesthetic ideology. At the same time, the argument is meant to deepen our knowledge of the Gothic tropes in Burke's writings. This, I will suggest, extends our understanding of the way conservative ideology conceptualizes order and the threats to that order, an understanding which became and remains a common feature in bourgeois political discourse. Finally, the chapter will link Burke's use of the monstrous to the place of the dead in his thought, a link which will then open the door for a comparative exploration of similar themes within the work of Marx and the fascist tradition in the following chapters.

A sublime revolution?

Early in his *Reflections* Burke describes the French Revolution as 'the most astonishing thing that has hitherto happened in the world'.[11] His recognition of such astonishment picks up on comments he had made earlier in 1789 regarding the Revolution. In a letter of 9 August 1789, for example, he had noted 'our astonishment at the wonderful Spectacle which is exhibited in a Neighbouring and rival Country . . . England gazing with astonishment at a French struggle for Liberty'.[12] And in a letter of November 1789 to Charles-Jean-François Depont, generally taken to be a first and sketchy outline of what would become the *Reflections*, he is found commenting on 'the astonishing scene now displayed in France'.[13] And he repeats the point in his much later *Letters on a Regicide Peace* of 1795–7: the Revolution 'has astonished, terrified, and almost overpowered Europe', and one can only be doubly astonished by the fact that there are those who do not feel resentment at the 'monstrous compound' before them.[14] Burke's account of the monstrosity that is emerging in France is thus clearly connected to the astonishment he is experiencing, and he assumes others are experiencing, at the spectacle.

To make sense of this astonishment we need to backtrack slightly into Burke's *Philosophical Enquiry into the Origin of our Ideas of the Sublime and Beautiful* (1757), where he first utilizes the notion of astonishment.

> The passion caused by the great and sublime in *nature*, when those causes operate most powerfully, is Astonishment; and astonishment is that state of the soul, in which all its motions are suspended, with some degree of horror . . . Hence arises the great power of the sublime, that far from being produced by them, it anticipates our reasonings, and hurries us on by an irresistible force.[15]

Astonishment is the highest degree of the 'delightful' horror and terror which is the foundation of the sublime.[16] It is clear from this that Burke's notion of astonishment is intimately connected to the question of fear, horror and terror. The sublime is 'that state of the soul, in which all its motions are suspended, with some degree of horror' while 'delightful horror' is 'the most genuine effect, and truest test of the sublime'. The sublime is on the side of novelty in the sense that it generates feelings of dread, and in particular the greatest dread – the fear of death. Elsewhere the 'delightful horror' of the sublime is described as 'a sort of tranquility tinged with terror'; 'whatever therefore is terrible . . . is sublime too'.[17] Burke makes a point of spelling out the idea that 'terror is in all cases . . . the ruling principle of the sublime' by pointing to the affinity between these ideas in a number of languages:

> Terror is in all cases whatsoever, either more openly or latently the ruling principle of the sublime. Several languages bear a strong testimony to the affinity of these ideas. They frequently use the same word, to signify indifferently the modes of astonishment or admiration and those of terror. Θάμβος is in greek, either fear or wonder; δεινός is terrible or respectable; αἰδέω, to reverence or to fear. *Vereor* in latin, is what αἰδέω is in greek. The Romans used the verb *stupeo*, a term which strongly marks the state of an astonished mind, to express the effect either of simple fear, or of astonishment; the word *attonitus*, (thunderstruck) is equally expressive of the alliance of these ideas; and do not the french *etonnement*, and the english *astonishment* and *amazement*, point out as clearly the kindred emotions which attend fear and wonder?[18]

Part of the difference between the sublime and the beautiful is thus that, despite having a variety of causes, such as vastness, silence, obscurity, solitude and power, the sublime has the capacity to astonish us, a capacity rooted in its connection with horror and fear.

In contrast, beauty is a quality fundamentally different to the sublime. Where sublime objects and actions impress with their power, loftiness and nobility, instilling astonishment, reverence and respect, beautiful objects 'induce in us a sense of affection and tenderness', or love; where sublime objects are solid, massive and rugged, beautiful objects are small, light, delicate and polished; where sublime virtues are strong and great, beautiful virtues are soft and subordinate. Thus the great virtues such as fortitude, justice and wisdom tend to be 'political and military', while the subordinate virtues, such as compassion

and kindness, are 'domestic'.[19] This plays on Burke's attempt to distinguish the sublime from the beautiful in terms of the way in which
the characteristics of a thing or activity give rise to feelings of pleasure
or pain by impinging on the mind by way of the senses. 'Whatever is
fitted in any sort to excite the ideas of pain, and danger, that is to say,
whatever is in any sort terrible, or is conversant about terrible objects,
or operates in a manner analogous to terror, is a source of the
sublime.'[20] The idea of pain is thus the strongest and most delightful
emotion which the mind is capable of feeling, and the grounds of the
sublime.

Now, although this argument is at one level pitched as a general
account of fear and pain, at another level it is distinctively political. 'I
know of nothing sublime which is not some modification of power. And
this branch rises as naturally as the other two branches, from terror,
the common stock of every thing that is sublime.'[21] But if it is distinctively political – if, that is, the sublime is always some modification
of power connected in some way to terror or horror – then an
important question emerges: can the horror or terror of a revolution
be sublime?

Tom Furniss has pointed out that, although the political project of
the *Enquiry* resides in its contribution to a debate which acted as a
means of authenticating the political and economic project of the
rising middle class, the sublime is not reducible to any single political
position concerning the form of political power.[22] On the one hand it
is potentially a source of tyranny in the guise of 'despotic governments
which are founded on the passions of men, and principally upon the
passion of fear'. Yet on the other hand Burke makes far more general
claims about the sublime nature of power: 'the power which arises
from institution in kings and commanders, has the same connection
with terror'. Thus 'sovereigns are frequently addressed with the title of
dread majesty',[23] and laws should possess 'salutary terrors'.[24] From
this it is clear that, as Furniss points out, the sublime cannot be un-
problematically resorted to as a way of distinguishing legitimate or
illegitimate forms of power.[25] Moreover, there are moments, such as
when Burke quotes from Milton's analysis of Satan ('here is a very
noble picture . . .'), when the *Enquiry* could be read as celebrating a
revolutionary sublime.[26] Similarly, the language of terror and horror
Burke uses in discussing the sublime reappears throughout his account
of the Revolution, in which we are constantly confronted by terrors
and horrors: the new government 'fills us with horror', we 'turn away

with horror', our minds 'are purified by terror' and so on.[27] Since
terror is either openly or latently the ruling principle of the sublime, it
does not seem unreasonable to assume that the revolutionary terror
unleashed in France could be thought of as sublime. His description of
central ancien regime figures such as Marie Antoinette as beautiful
and his accusation that the revolutionaries have stripped away all the
sentiments, pleasing illusions and decent drapery which serve to
'beautify and soften private society' would also suggest that the
Revolution might in some way be sublime.[28]

Thus it might be argued that Burke comes to figure the French
Revolution as potentially producing 'the effect of the sublime in the
highest degree',[29] or that 'for Burke revolutionary terror is itself a kind
of sublimity'.[30] In other words, 'one solution to the confrontation with
this unthinkable phenomenon, the French Revolution, was [for Burke]
to fit it into the framework of aesthetic categories . . . Burke's imagery
of revolution in fact came from . . . the terrible of the sublime'.[31] Since
images of fear permeate Burke's works, and since the monster appears
to incarnate fear as such, it would seem that it is here that the monster
needs to be situated: the revolutionary horror is both monstrous and
sublime. This would also tally with Burke's suggestion in the *Enquiry*
that ghosts, goblins and harpies affect minds with fear and terror.[32]
Yet the general consensus among commentators is that for obvious
ideological reasons Burke has to hold back from interpreting the
Revolution as an instance of the sublime. The astonishment which is
celebrated in the *Enquiry* as the source of the sublime has become in
the *Reflections* an astonishment at another sort of horror, one which is
no longer sublime. Burke therefore aims to refute implicitly any claim
that the Revolution might be either sublime or beautiful by attempting
to show instead that it is merely barbaric terror, especially compared
to the way the ancien regime and the British constitution are thought
to be endowed with 'sublime principles'. The British constitution, for
example, 'is tempered with an awful gravity', while the state should be
consecrated and treated with 'pious awe and trembling solicitude'.
Similarly, it is 'settled and recognized authority' that is expected to be
treated with 'awe and reverence'.[33] At the same time, his references to
horror in the *Reflections* are no longer associated with the sublime but
with disgust,[34] abominations,[35] shame,[36] scorn,[37] and institutions such
as the Bastille under Louis XVI;[38] the revolutionaries are attacked for
seeing the nobility as 'objects of horror'.[39] Terror is likewise associated
not with the sublime but with barbarism, evil and the bayonet.[40]

In general, commentators have therefore concluded that in the *Reflections* Burke seems concerned that the sublime is moving in an unanticipated direction, from those awesome and revered forms of traditional power to the revolutionary movement. He therefore has to rethink the sublime such that it would appear that the terror and horror of the Revolution constitute a kind of *false sublime*. Burke now appears to be saying that the true sublime in government is a mixture of fear and awe or admiration, whereas the false sublime is a perversion of this and generates only a barbaric and grotesque energy.[41] It is here, I believe, that we can begin to identify and explain the roots of Burke's use of the monster metaphor.

While the monstrous society may initially appear to possess the kind of terror or horror that Burke associates with the sublime in his *Enquiry*, it fails to satisfy an important criteria in Burke's account of the sublime. In the *Enquiry* Burke asks himself an obvious question: how can terror or horror be delightful? 'If the sublime is built on terror, or some passion like it, which has pain for its object; it is previously proper to enquire how any species of delight can be derived from a cause so apparently contrary to it.' On this score, he highlights what to him is a fundamental dimension of the relationship between terror and the sublime: 'when danger or pain *press too nearly*, they are incapable of giving any delight, and are simply terrible; but *at certain distances*, and with certain modifications, they may be, and they are delightful'. Thus while on the one hand Burke connects the sublime with the terror and fear of death, on the other he insists that only in the safety enjoyed when the danger and pain do not 'press too close' is the sublime truly experienced. It is 'the removal of pain or danger' that becomes crucial to distinguishing the sublime from the 'simply terrible'.[42] Sublime delight occurs only when one enjoys the terror or fear from a position of safety. Terror can produce delight only when it does not press too nearly; the false sublime would thus equate with pure unmediated terror. In the case of revolutionary France, the terror clearly 'pressed too nearly' and lacked a 'certain distance'. The *Reflections*, it must be remembered, were intended as a response to those Englishmen who might see revolutionary France as a 'model held up to ourselves'[43] – to those who might move, that is, from being spectators to being active participants in a revolutionary politics. In this case, the necessary *distancing* required for the sublime to be operative disappears, and the terror can no longer be enjoyed from a position of safety. On these initial grounds we can say that Burke invokes the monster as a way of disengaging the sublime from the horror and terror emerging in France. The kind of order emerging was less a form of delightful dread and more a form of barbarous horror, breaking with the necessary distancing and pressing far too nearly. The terror emerging across the Channel was thus less sublime than monstrous.

If this argument has any substance then we should expect to find in Burke's texts an increased use of the monster as a means of ideologically interpellating the French Revolution throughout the 1790s as 'the Terror' becomes clearer. And this is indeed what we find. In his writings of 1791, for example, we find comments on 'the monster of a commonwealth' and 'the monster . . . having torn the womb it came from'.[44] This becomes a key theme in his *Letters on a Regicide Peace*, which repeat some of the comments of the *Reflections* concerning, for example, France as a 'monstrous Tragi-comedy', but also contain references to the 'monstrous shapes' of 'this monster of a State', regicide France as 'the mother of monsters, more prolifick than the country of old called *ferax monstrorum*', and the revolutionaries themselves as monsters desecrating and degrading the state.[45] In the French regicide republic, Burke argues,

> we have, formed, a new, unlooked-for, monstrous, heterogeneous alliance; a double-natured Monster; Republic above and Monarchy below. There is no Centaur of fiction, no poetic Satyr of the Woods; nothing short of the Hieroglyphick Monsters of Aegypt. Dog in Head and Man in Body, that can give an idea of it. None of these things can subsist in nature; so at least it is thought. But the moral world admits Monsters, which the physical rejects.[46]

Likewise, 'the grim Moloch of Regicide' brought about by the 'revolution harpies' and 'nefarious monsters of France' is nothing less than a 'monstrous compound' culminating in monstrous acts of cannibalism.[47] In 'A Letter to a Noble Lord' from 1796 he quotes Milton on the generation of 'monstrous, prodigious things' out of 'chaotick anarchy', and then cites several lines from Virgil:

> Tristius haud illis monstrum, nec saevior ulla.
> Pestis, & ira Deûm Stygiis sese extulit undis.
> Virginei volucrum vultus; faedissima ventris
> Proluvies; uncaeque manus; & pallida semper
> Ora fame –

> Monsters more fierce offended Heav'n ne'er sent
> From hell's abyss, for human punishment:
> With virgin faces, but with wombs obscene
> Foul paunches, and with ordure unclean;
> With claws for hands, and looks forever lean –

Burke comments:

> Here the Poet breaks the line, because he (and that He is Virgil) had not verse or language to describe that monster even as he had conceived her. Had he lived to our time, he would have been more overpowered with the reality than he was with the imagination. Virgil only knew the horror of the times before him. Had he lived to see the Revolutionists and Constitutionalists of France, he would have had more horrid and disgusting features of his harpies to describe, and more frequent failures in the attempt to describe them.[48]

Stricken by such fear, Burke castigates both the French population and English admirers of the Revolution for being 'not in the least disgusted or discouraged by the monstrous evils' carried out by 'this monster of a Directory', and dismisses those who place our hopes 'in the moderation and virtue of the most atrocious monsters that have ever disgraced and plagued mankind'. He even on occasion describes particular individuals of this 'union of characters, monstrous as it seems', as individual monsters.[49]

It is clear, then, that the monster features heavily in Burke's writings on France, that it plays an increasing role in Burke's arguments as the French Revolution progresses and that part of the reason for Burke's use of the metaphor of the monster lies in his work on the sublime and the need to protect the sublime from being associated with the Revolution: the revolutionary dream of reason brings forth monsters. Burke's aesthetic ideology, in other words, pushes him to configure the Revolution as monstrous. But an obvious question to ask at this point is: why? Is there a more political reason beyond the 'false sublime' that pushes Burke into engaging the monster metaphor? Any answers to these questions will necessarily be speculative. In what follows I suggest that one source of Burke's use of the idea of monstrosity is a generalized fear of 'the multitude' and what later becomes known as mass action. The extent to which the writings of major bourgeois thinkers in the tradition of the 'history of political thought' were shaped by fear of the multitude is well known. What I am doing here is exploring the way that the developing 'conservative' strand of bourgeois ideology, exemplified by Burke, was likewise shaped by the same fear. But I shall also suggest that implicit in this fear was a sense of a new collective force emerging on the historical landscape: the proletariat. It is precisely this fear of both the multitude/mass (that is, 'mob', as we shall see) in general and the working class in particular that comes to play a key role in bourgeois ideology thereafter.

Mobs and monsters

Cultural historians have shown that, as the first attempt to systematize a connection between sublimity and terror, Burke's *Philosophical Enquiry* helped launch the Gothic novel, which itself became part of the tradition of the sublime. Gothic novelists of the late eighteenth century and scholars of the Gothic novel ever since have consulted Burke's *Philosophical Enquiry* as if it were a storehouse of approved terrors. It has even been suggested that Burke was the founder of political Gothic and that his portrayal of the French revolutionaries is startling in its Gothic conventionality.[50] 'Gothic' is of course hardly the most subtle of concepts. But if, as is commonly assumed, the 'Gothic' refers us to the question of the extra-rational and encourages us to enlarge our sense of reality and its impact on human being,[51] and if, as the Marquis de Sade once commented, Gothic literature was 'the inevitable result of the revolutionary shocks which all of Europe has suffered',[52] then perhaps there is some political insight to be had from exploring the monster. As Michel Foucault has suggested, the Gothic is a form of political fiction as well as science fiction, in that Gothic novels focus on the abuse of power and tend to reactivate a whole 'knowledge' about feudalism, inscribing in the imagination a knowledge of a supposedly golden age of right, history and politics.[53] In this sense it might just be worth unpicking Burke's 'Gothic conventionality' a little in order to make a more political point. As De Bruyn puts it:

> In an age when unprecedented historical events were rapidly overtaking the strangest of gothic fancies, to say nothing of previous historical and polit-ical orthodoxy, journalists and political commentators such as Edmund Burke increasingly recognized in the gothic mode a means of apprehending or conceptualizing the bewildering sequence of public events unfolding before

their eyes. The gothic served for them as a metaphor or narrative thread to enable the writing of new kinds of political and journalistic discourse.[54]

David Punter has thus argued that the Gothic has always contained 'a very intense, if displaced, engagement with political and social problems'.[55] The reason why the Gothic could perform this function lies in the fact that, as José Monleón has shown, 'one of the main features of Gothic literature is precisely its defense of order and its negation of arbitrary rule'.[56] Consequently, one of the sources of the anxiety and foreboding in Gothic fiction is a deep-seated fear of radical social upheaval and, of course, a longing for the golden age in which such upheaval was supposedly impossible.

How then can we situate Burke's 'monster' in this context? Two preliminary remarks concerning the monster in general need to be made here. On the one hand, part of the original frame of reference of the monster is natural history. The long intellectual history of reflection on the monster, traceable at least to Democritus and Aristotle, centres very much on physical 'defects', relative ages of reproduction, the extent to which individual humans and animals resemble their parents, and so on – 'natural' monstrosities in other words.[57] This interest intensifies during the early modern period, for example in Francis Bacon's call for a study to categorize 'errors of nature, freaks and monsters', and culminates in the eighteenth-century focus on (or perhaps obsession with) identifying and delineating the boundaries of the human. An offshoot of the attempt at classifying the different 'races' of mankind and to consider which of them were suitable for the status of citizen was an attempt to differentiate the human from the non-human – or monstrous. Hence Linnaeus's final double-column scheme separating *homo sapiens* from *homo monstruosus*. On the other hand, the other original frame of reference of the monster is law. As a breach of natural limits and/or a dangerous mixing (of bodies, species, sexes or forms), the monster was also thought to breach legal classifications: it was/is law that had to decide the nature of the being in question. By the eighteenth century, then, the monster had become the point at which nature and law were joined.[58]

The basis of this original juridico-natural frame of reference was order: natural order on the one side, legal order on the other. It is in this context that the monster becomes a problem. Analyses of the monster tend to suggest that, culturally speaking, monsters are defined by their categorical ambiguity and troubling *mobility*.

A monster is that which cannot be placed in any of the taxonomic schemes devised by the human mind to understand and to order nature. It exceeds the very basis of classification, language itself: it is an excess of signifi-cation, a strange byproduct or leftover of the process of making and meaning. It is an imaginary being who comes to life in language and, once having done so, cannot be eliminated from language.[59]

The difficulty in categorizing the monster in the 'order of things' – the order of natural things and the order of legal things – makes it a harbinger of category crisis. The monster's mobility disrupts the usual rules of interaction, occupying an essentially fluid site where despite its otherness it cannot be entirely separated from nature and man. As simultaneously inside and outside, the monster disrupts the politics of identity and the security of borders. The monster and its mobility thus represents something crucial: disorder. The monster is, in essence, a threat to order.

But 'order' is a deeply ideological concept.[60] Riding on the back of an implied connection between natural and political order, the idea of monstrosity that emerges in the eighteenth century was less juridico-natural and more socio-political: a monstrosity of socio-political conduct rather than a monstrosity of nature.[61] It is for this reason that Slavoj i ek describes the monster as the 'object' through which the citizen-subject of the Enlightenment acquired its positive dynamic.[62] But the point is that the monster's juridicio-natural transgression was easily reconsidered in terms of political transgression, generating what I am suggesting we think of as a political teratology. Since, for Burke, 'good order is the foundation of all good things'[63] it should not surprise us that he presents threats to order in terms of their monstrosity.

This connects with the organic tropes in Burke's writings. As is well known, Burke's politics plays heavily on the ideas of an organic order and the body politic which together generate a range of rhetorical devices in his work – heads, bodies and limbs; plagues, purges and panaceas; cancers, contagions and quarantines – which serve to naturalize traditional order in general and the ancien regime in par-ticular in terms of the corporatist fantasy of a body/society without conflict.[64] The qualification 'monster' plays heavily on these rhetorical devices, partly because the monster runs contrary to nature but also because the qualification must by definition be reserved for organic beings.[65] The definition of monster must include its nature as a living being or, as we shall see in a theme that will begin to resonate through this book, its nature as a *once-living* and yet *not fully dead* being. Burke's use of the metaphor therefore performs a useful ideological function in terms of his organic analogy, reaffirming the illusion of organic and political order. Behind the representation of the revolutionary events as monstrous is the assumption that organic and political order are one and the same. The unease produced by the monster is thus a form of dis-ease. Revolutionary France is monstrous because it is 'out of nature' – nothing less than 'a contrivance of nature'.[66] Just as a creature which is 'Dog in Head and Man in Body' cannot subsist in nature, so any such political 'double-natured Monster', such as one which is 'Republic above and Monarchy below' also should not be allowed to exist in the moral universe. 'But', Burke laments, 'the moral world admits Monsters, which the physical rejects.'[67] (Chris Baldick has also pointed out that it is symptomatic of Burke's argument concerning the 'monstrous compound' that France was becoming that he stresses the interest in scientific experiment among the radicals of the time. For Burke the monstrosity was partly a result of the excessive and obsessive interest in experiment, computing, sorcery, alchemy and chemistry on the part of the revolutionaries.[68]) If teratology was born of the meeting between comparative anatomy and embryology,[69] then it might be said that *political* teratology has a remarkable presence in the organic and biological tropes used in political thinking. The general point is that, just as the natural order is supposedly threatened by the various monsters it sometimes spawns, so the socio-political order appears to be threatened by the various monsters it spawns. Of course, for Burke the socio-political order he is defending is (in some sense) a natural order, and on these grounds the monster metaphor makes perfect sense. His monster is thus called upon to legitimize an intuitive vision of life in which 'natural' order appears to be threatened by 'artificial' monstrosities. To develop the argument here I will suggest that the monster Burke so feared at this stage possessed such categorical ambiguity and troubling mobility, and was harbinger of such a category crisis, that it had not yet been properly named and rendered an integral part of the social order. It had not yet been named: as the proletariat. Why the proletariat?[70]

In the third of his *Letters on a Regicide Peace* (from 1797) Burke suddenly shifts his focus to the question of whether 'the present war' is the cause of the high price of provisions during 1796. This allows him to introduce the question of the labouring class and the level of wages.

> On the whole, I am satisfied, that the humblest class, and that class which touches the most nearly on the lowest, out of which it is continually emerging, and to which it is continuously falling, receives far more from publick impositions than it pays. That class receives two million sterling annually from the classes above it. It pays no such amount towards any publick contribution.[71]

Burke's concern here follows from his lengthy memorandum to William Pitt from two years previously (his essay 'Thoughts and Details on Scarcity' of 1795), in which he had railed against state subsidies for the labouring class during a period of poor harvests and even famine. But his digression into the pricing of provisions and public finance is also symptomatic of an interest in the question of class which runs through Burke's work.

It might be said that Burke's concern in both the *Letters on a Regicide Peace* and 'Thoughts and Details on Scarcity' is with the necessity for the labouring class to continue to labour. But Burke's essentially bourgeois political economy, in which wage labour by the bulk of the population is assumed to be a necessity, is far from uncommon for the time. What is distinct about Burke's argument is that it also builds on the class dynamic immanent in the *Enquiry*. For Burke, the experience of the sublime is confined to a cultivated few. The closest the labouring mass get to the experience of the sublime is in nothing less than their labour. 'As common labour, which is a mode of pain, is the exercise of the grosser, a mode of terror is the exercise of the finer parts of the system.'[72] Thus as well as being the foundation of both the wealth of nations and the order and discipline of the working class, labour also figures as a poor person's version of the sublime.[73] Burke's concern is that the labouring class will wish to give up the pain of labour and thus lose its fear or, in Burke's aesthetic terms, its reverence and awe. In so doing, it becomes nothing but a mob.

Burke had already commented on the 'horrors of mob-government' in his *Thoughts on the Cause of the Present Discontents*: 'Unable to rule the multitude, they endeavour to raise divisions amongst them. One mob is hired to destroy another; a procedure which at once encourages the boldness of the populace, and justly increases their discontent.' But the point there was that an unruly multitude/mob can be used by political factions.[74] In the *Reflections* the concern is with this 'boldness' and the targets to which it might be directed. One problem with revolutionary fervour identified by Burke is that it undermines 'the principles of natural subordination' which are the grounds of discipline for the mob.

> They [the mob] must respect that property of which they cannot partake. They must labour to obtain what by labour can be obtained; and when they find, as they commonly do, the success disproportioned to the endeavour, they must be taught their consolation in the final proportions of eternal justice.[75]

Thus the reason Burke is left implicitly bemoaning a false sublime in the *Reflections* lies in his perception of the *political mobilization* of the labouring class during the revolutionary fervour. And what in turn Burke fears most from this revolutionary fervour is the loss of reverence and fear on the part of the labouring mass of the population. Such a loss would result not just in a threat to the established order – 'Is it in destroying and pulling down that skill is displayed? Your mob can do this as well at least as your assemblies'[76] – but to the continuation of settled property ownership too; a key difference between 1688 and 1789 is precisely that in the former no mobs marched through the streets with the heads of gentlemen 'stuck upon spears'.[77]

Tom Furniss and Frances Ferguson have suggested that whereas the mob is immanent within Burke's theory of the sublime, in the *Reflections* it has become properly mobile, and it is this mobility that undermines any possibility of it being the 'true' sublime.[78] I would argue that the 'mobility' and thus ungovernability of the mob turns out to represent rather too much sublimity for Burke's taste, to the extent that it becomes merely terrible. 'Mob', it should be recalled, is an abbreviation of the Latin *mobile vulgus*, developed by the ruling class in the eighteenth century as a code for the poor and thus the emergent working class. (Burke half-apologizes for using it: 'excuse the term, it is still in use here'.[79]) In particular, it became code for *disorderliness* and *mobility* (that is, mobility *as* disorderliness) on the part of the labouring class – as, for example, in Adam Smith's comments on 'mobbish and disorderly assemblies' in the *Wealth of Nations*.[80] Much has been made of Burke's description of the mob or lower orders as a 'swinish multitude': should the revolutionaries succeed, he suggests, learning and its natural guardians 'will be cast into the mire, and trodden down under the hoofs of a swinish multitude'.[81] But we need to read Burke as suggesting that the mob is not only mobile and thus open to mobilization, ungovernable, swinish and all in all terrible – it is also monstrous. Indeed, the monstrosity of the mob lies in its mobility and disorderliness; its terrible 'mobbishness' is the crux of its monstrosity.

In employing the figure of the monster in this way Burke was building on an established tradition in the ideological strategies of the ruling class. Historians such as Christopher Hill, Peter Linebaugh and Marcus Rediker have shown at length the extent to which one particular monster, the many-headed hydra, figures as an ideological ploy in ruling class discourse. In text after text the working class appears as a 'hydra of misrule', a monster which grows new heads when one of its existing heads is lopped off. The myth of the many-headed hydra was thus intended to capture the difficulty of imposing order on increasingly global and mobile systems of labour.[82] Despite focusing on one particular monstrous form, Hill, Linebaugh and Rediker identify a key aspect of political teratology more generally: it is centrally concerned with the question of class. As such, one might extend the kind of political teratology explored by these writers well beyond the hydra to many other forms of monster. One might, for example, trace the connection between Thomas Hobbes's figure of rebellion in the form of the monstrous Behemoth and his concern over the emergence from feudal order of a 'dissolute condition of master-lesse men, without subjection to Lawes, and a coercive Power to tye their hands'.[83] Burke's adoption of the idiom of monstrosity was thus, on the one hand, hardly new. Yet on the other hand Burke is writing during the period in which the Gothic literary form had become predominant. I noted earlier that the Gothic might be thought of as activating in the political imagination a 'knowledge' about a golden age. But we must also note that the Gothic also 'occupies the first stage of the creation of the modern bourgeois society, that is, roughly the period between 1760 and 1815'.[84] In other words the emergence and rise of the Gothic from the 1760s coincides with the beginning of the industrial revolution – the beginning of a period of intensive capital accumulation and thus the gradual emergence of an industrial working class. I suggest that it is in the context of this emerging class formation – a confused, complex, heavily overdetermined process, but a process of class formation nonetheless – that Burke's use of the monster trope and, concomitantly, the class politics of Burke's aesthetic ideology and political teratology needs to be understood.

Now, this argument cannot be made without a couple of important qualifying comments. First, we must note with C. B. Macpherson that

'Burke was not a nineteenth-century historian' and thus 'did not see modern history in terms of class conquests of power'.[85] Because Burke simultaneously favoured both a 'free market' economy and yet wished to defend substantial settled property he did not see the Revolution as a transfer of power to a substantial bourgeoisie or as removing feudal obstacles to the development of a fully fledged bourgeois order in France and thus Europe as a whole. It would be unreasonable to read Burke as having a clear and coherent class conception of the Revolution. Moreover, and secondly, one has to recognize that 'the proletariat' as such was hardly fully formed at this time – it would be another fifty or so years before it would emerge as a historical actor of any substantive political force. Even Marx's announcement in 1844 that what is needed for communism is a class with radical chains is immediately followed by the observation that the proletariat is only now coming into being.[86]

In other words, it would have to be said that the 'class' nature of the monster was hardly clear to Burke, nor could it have been. And yet it is in part precisely this lack of clarity which encourages Burke to use the notion of the monstrous – he simply has no other way of thinking through such an as yet unidentifiable and yet threatening political force. Since at this point the proletariat had not fully become 'the proletariat' (that is, had not become a fully fledged class on the historical stage), a conceptual vacuum existed which Burke filled with the concept of the monster. The classification 'monster' was Burke's way of imagining the unimaginable – of filling the empty conceptual space that would only later become occupied by the proletariat. The posters which advertised theatrical adaptations of *Frankenstein* during Mary Shelley's lifetime usually left a blank space opposite the name of the actor who played the monster. Shelley rather liked this, as she thought it a creative way of 'naming the unnameable'.[87] We might think of Burke's 'monster' as precisely a way of 'naming' what was then politically unnameable.[88] Because the enemy is not yet recognized as a class in and of itself, or even a class recognizable as such, it is inter-pellated as an unnameable thing. Burke's joint preoccupation with the mob class and his invocation of the metaphor of the monster are two of the complex of terms, including 'swinish multitude', developed in ruling-class ideology through the eighteenth century as a way of identifying and politically labeling the nascent and thus far un-nameable proletariat. Or, to put it in the aesthetic terms of the *Philosophical Enquiry*, it was a way for Burke to identify the multitude as no longer awe-ful, but as now merely awful.

The sheer awfulness of the monstrous class mob helps explain the emotional force and political intensity of Burke's descriptions of the revolutionary events in France. Although commentators have often queried this force and intensity, given the fact that Burke did not experience the events in France at first hand, the point is that Burke's response to them is heavily dependent on his experience of the Wilkite disturbances and the Gordon Riots, not only because in the case of the latter his own life had been threatened, but because of his conviction, attested to by his parliamentary speeches of the early 1790s, that these events were all connected. Richard Price, whose sermon to the Revolution Society was the immediate cause of Burke's *Reflections*, was a protégé of Lord Shelburne, whom Burke suspected of having fomented the Gordon Riots. As O'Brien puts it, 'Burke's feelings about what he read of the excesses of the Paris revolutionary mob in 1789 blended, in his imagination, with his still vivid memories of that London Protestant mob of nine years before.'[89] Hence his exaggerated characterization of both rioters and revolutionaries as a frenzied mob or fanatical monster.

None of this argument is intended to imply that the French Revolution was some kind of proletarian uprising, for that would clearly be absurd. Nor is it to downplay the enormous political, social and historical differences between the Gordon Riots, the French Revolution and the later political actions of the organized proletariat. And as I have suggested, it is also not to imply that the proletariat was clearly identifiable to Burke (or anyone else) in this period. Rather, it is to suggest that Burke's fear lay in any large-scale movement of the 'multitude' – 'the people' of/from the lower orders appearing as an active historical subject on the world stage – and that *implicit* in this conception of the multitude was the emergent modern proletariat. Burke's use of the idiom of monstrosity can thus be traced to the new processes of industrial society then emerging and, concomitantly, the new forms of mobility – in both the individual and collective sense – exercised by workers. In utilizing the monster this way Burke therefore seeks to score a political as well as an aesthetic point. What was at stake in the Revolution was nothing less than a monstrous movement creating a monstrous society. It is impossible to believe that Burke did not know that 'monster' is derived from a complex of related terms: *monstrare* meaning 'to show forth', *monstra* and *monestrum* meaning to warn or show, *monstrum* meaning 'that which reveals', or 'that which warns', and *monere* meaning 'to warn'. Similarly, the word

Aristotle and the Greeks use for abnormal forms is *teras*, meaning a warning or portent, giving rise in the early modern period to the possibility of a *teratology*. The conservative function of Burke's use of the monstrous, then, lies in its warning or demonstration of what to avoid. Burke's use of the monster trope in part plays on the idea that the monstrous mob currently dominating the historic stage is a sign: a political teratology warning of things to come.

Like many political tropes (and many political myths), the 'monster' in this political teratology oscillates wildly between movements, forces, institutions and processes. But despite such oscillation, the trope centred on a historic moment and movement in which 'the people' was beginning to appear on the historic stage having shaken off its reverence and awe. In grappling ideologically with such a moment and movement Burke developed a political rhetoric which became a standard device of bourgeois ideology. It is a rhetoric which avoids talking of class directly and instead tends to employ either insults (the swinish multitude), or euphemisms (hairdressers), or both. It also tends to employ abstractions – the mob or, of course, the monster. Attending the British Conservative Party conference in 1984, Sarah Benton tried to discuss with delegates the reasons why they were conservative. Listening to them reveal some of the usual hatreds found on the right – for Marxists and muggers, subversives and the 1960s, blacks and foul-mouthed women – Benton was drawn to one conclusion: 'no one talked of class'. Rather, 'anyone could join the court of the great and the good, mingle with them on equal terms; feel . . . that they were part of the embodiment of a mystical national good'.[90] Instead of class, what gets conjured up is some other form of enemy, a process which, as Benton puts it, 'can only derive coherence from the conjuring up of the Alien, a force whose shape you never quite see but which lurks in every unlit space ready to destroy you; and is incubated, unnoticed, in the healthy body politic'. The idea that there was some alien force within the body politic was a prevalent theme at the time, from Margaret Thatcher's comments on the 'enemy within' (namely, workers organized into trade unions) to the recognition by commentators such as Benton. Laura Mulvey, for example, comments: 'Like the Frankenstein monster, the miners struggled for control of their own story, and like the monster, were cast simultaneously as evil and tragic.'[91] I am suggesting that such an idea has a very long history: as long as conservatism itself. Burke's invocation of the monstrous might thus be thought of as one of his most important contributions to bourgeois ideology in general and its conservative strand in particular. Stephen King has suggested that, culturally speaking, 'monstrosity fascinates us because it appeals to the conservative Republican in a three-piece suit who resides within all of us'. Playing on a fear of disorder means that 'it is not the physical or mental aberration in itself which horrifies us, but rather the lack of order which these aberrations seem to imply'.[92] One of conservatism's major contributions was to turn such fears into political drives. For the fear of 'the monstrous' became central to the conservative imagination thereafter, broadening out to become a key ideological trope in identifying the 'enemies of order' within bourgeois political thinking.

Somewhere within Burke's use of the metaphor was a fearful sense of the material force that would eventually shake and shape European history. But as Timothy Beal notes, making enemies into monsters is a kind of conjuring, and conjuring is always risky because it runs the risk of producing more than one bargains for. That is, it runs the risk of more than simply marking out a clear enemy. 'Insofar as . . . monsters are the otherworldly within the worldly, such conjuring also endows the enemy with a kind of supernatural, primordial, mysterious otherness, an agency that resists being reduced to an easy target, and that never stays down for long.'[93] And this is precisely how the working class comes to figure in the conservative political imagination – or perhaps that should be 'nightmare'. In setting up the 'monstrous' in this way Burke thereby inaugurated what became one of the core features of the conservative nightmare: the monster of mob rule.

'Monster' and 'mob' are of course ambiguous terms. But the ambiguity probably assists in the ideological role they play in some political arguments. Giving some kind of name to an otherwise invisible adversary – naming the unnameable – is crucial to the political construction of social fear which drives conservatism as a political ideology and strategy. But not only conservatism, for as we shall see in Chapter 3, conservatism here shares with fascism a fundamental psychic trope which easily doubles up as a reactionary political tool. Scratch a conservative (and, as we shall see, a fascist) and the fear is always there, just below the surface. 'Journey into the mind of the conservative. What you will encounter is fear. Fear of crime. Fear of enemies. Fear of change. Fear of people not exactly like them. And, of course, fear of losing any money on anything.'[94] Acting out its inherent structure of aggression, conservatism blatantly draws on the violence which underpins power as such, mobilizing fear for its own politics of order. Those Marxists and muggers, anarchists and liberals, young blacks and single mothers are all configured as monsters existing in the darkness of history, but whose existence helps keep alive that fear without which there can be no rule.[95] They also want everyone else to share and act on this fear. 'Be afraid, be very afraid – and trust us to protect you' is conservatism's bottom line. Also, as we shall see with fascism, the conservative does not wish for the monster to truly disappear from the world, but merely for his 'own' people to take over and hold on to the reins.

Reconciliation; or the authority of the dead

One of the better known features of Burke's *Reflections* is the way in which it articulates a political vision founded on tradition, the established order, the hereditary principle and the past in general. Against the supposed 'favourableness of present times' in which enlightened theorists 'despise all their predecessors', Burke proposes 'canonized forefathers' for whom 'a politic caution, a guarded circumspection, a moral rather than a complexional timidity were among the ruling principles'; against those who 'despise experience', Burke proposes finding 'in history a great volume . . . unrolled for our instruction'; against those who seek to level and equalize, Burke proposes 'old establishments' which are 'tried by the effects'; against those who seek the 'right to choose our governors' Burke offers 'the sacredness of an hereditary principle of succession'; against the new cult of liberty Burke proposes the tradition in which liberty was 'tempered with an awful gravity'.[96] All in all then, a preference for the past over the present: 'I set out with a perfect distrust of my own abilities; a total renunciation of every speculation of my own; and with a profound reverence for the wisdom of our ancestors.'[97]

His general position that reforms made in and to a state should be conducted 'upon the principle of reference to antiquity' makes antiquity a central theme and key rhetorical device throughout the text. The English are tied to the ancient nature of their rights and liberties embedded and embodied in the ancient constitution and corporations, a fact which provides the grounds for his advice that 'to make a revolution is to subvert the antient state of our country'.[98]

> Had you made it to be understood . . . that you were resolved to resume
> your ancient privileges, whilst you preserved the spirit of your ancient and
> your recent loyalty and honour; or, if diffident of yourselves, and not clearly
> discerning the almost obliterated constitution of your ancestors, you had
> looked to your neighbours in this land, who had kept alive the ancient
> principles and models of the old common law of Europe meliorated and
> adapted to its present state – by following wise examples you would have
> given new examples of wisdom to the world.[99]

The ancient is the 'compass to govern us', providing the foundations
of the constitution and law, simultaneously providing the 'permanent
sense of mankind' and the grounds for distinguishing between ourselves and strangers.[100] Even the *tyrants* of antiquity had some things
going for them, teaching us manners, providing the grounds for the
constitution and educating us in the defects of absolute democracy.[101]

Such arguments concerning the importance of tradition and the
sanctity of the ancient are now generally understood as providing the
first systematic formulation of one of the foundation stones of conservative thought: the purpose of conservatism is to conserve the
principles, wisdom and beauty of the past. My point here, however,
will be to suggest that Burke's (and conservatism's) assumptions, claims
and arguments are founded on a particular conception of the dead. A
sense of this was originally picked up by Thomas Paine. In his defence
of the rights of man Paine also saw himself as defending what he
thought of as the rights of the living over the claims of the dead.
Opposing 'the vanity and presumption of governing beyond the grave'
and the use of 'musty records and mouldy parchments to prove that
the rights of the living are lost', Paine insists that 'it is the living, and
not the dead, that are to be accommodated'. Laws must 'derive their
force from the consent of the living'. Thus Paine makes clear:

> as government is for the living, and not for the dead, it is the living only that
> has any right in it. That which may be thought right and found convenient
> in one age, may be thought wrong and found inconvenient in another. In
> such cases, Who is to decide, the living, or the dead?

As a consequence, he sees his response to Burke to be rooted in a
different conception of the living vis-à-vis the dead: 'I am contending
for the rights of the *living*, and against their being willed away, and
controlled and contracted for, by the manuscript assumed authority of

the dead; and Mr Burke is contending for the authority of the dead over the rights and freedom of the living.'[102] In a sense, Paine pre-empts some of Marx's formulations regarding the living and the dead, which I explore at length in Chapter 2. But Paine fails to grasp the fact that Burke's concern was less with the past and more to do with how the past links to the present and thus the future: 'people will not look forward to posterity, who never look backwards to their ancestors'. Paine's failure is important because it suggests a distinction between the living and the dead which is far too categorical and, if taken literally, actually *facilitates* the conservative attempt to trumpet the dead for the cause of conservatism. For in working with a simple distinction between a politics which values the dead to one which talks up the rights of the living, it leaves the dead to be appropriated for the conservative vision of posterity or, worse still, for another politics of the right. This claim can only be sustained as I develop the argument concerning the dead in Chapters 2 and 3. The remainder of this chapter, instead, focuses specifically on Burke.

Burke claims that society is a partnership 'not only between those who are living, but between those who are living, those who are dead, and those who are to be born'. This is the 'great primaeval contract of eternal society, linking the lower with the higher natures, connecting the visible and invisible world, according to a fixed compact sanctioned by the inviolable oath which holds all physical and all moral natures, each in their appointed place'. Society, then, is like all corporate bodies: eternal or immortal, and is so for the good of its members.[103] So when Burke writes about the vast libraries, ancient records and collections of artworks provided by landed property, what is at stake is nothing less than 'grand monuments of the dead', the purpose of which is to 'continue the regards and connexions of life beyond the grave'.[104] As such, the dead hold all the trumps. Even arguments are more convincing when they come from the dead. Reflecting in his *Thoughts on the Cause of the Present Discontents* on debates about the power of the Commons and constitutional reform he comments: 'Never has a subject been more amply and more learnedly handled, nor upon one side, in my opinion, more satis-factorily; they who are not convinced by what is written would not receive conviction *though one arose from the dead.*'[105] And when he praises the knowledge embodied in 'one old experienced peasant' compared to the 'enlightened', Burke quotes Cicero's report of a farmer's reply when asked why he labours: ' "Diis immortalibus sero"

[I sow for the immortal Gods], said an old Roman when he held one handle of the plough, whilst Death held the other.'[106] God, Death and the wisdom of old peasants: what more could a good conservative want?

Now, on an initial reading this conception of death and the socio-political importance of the past might appear at odds with part of the argument concerning the sublime. The sublime, recall, is on the side of novelty. But in the *Reflections* Burke appears to be stressing tradition rather than novelty, and the established against the original. As Furniss comments: 'if the *Enquiry* both champions the aesthetics of originality and individual experience and is itself a strong bid for originality, in the *Reflections* thirty-three years later Burke notoriously reverts to arguments from authority, from precedent, and from the documents of the dead'.[107] In the *Reflections*, in other words, the novelty of the sublime seems to have been displaced by the familiarity of the past, a familiarity associated, for a mixture of sentimental, historical and political reasons, with the dead. Yet this apparent disjunction between the two texts is in fact less of a disjunction than it at first appears, because the sublime, while associated with novelty, is also associated with death. For Burke, fear is 'an apprehension of pain or death' and the highest terror is the terror of death. 'The ideas of pain, and *above all of death*, are so very effecting, that whilst we remain in the presence of whatever is supposed to have the power of inflicting either, it is impossible to be perfectly free from terror.'[108] Death is thus the 'king of terrors' and pain its emissary.[109]

> As pain is stronger in its operation than pleasure, so death is in general a much more affecting idea than pain; because there are very few pains, however exquisite, which are not preferred to death; nay, what generally makes pain itself, if I may say so, more painful, is that it is considered as an emissary of this king of terrors.[110]

At the end of the *Enquiry* Burke for the second time cites Milton's comments on death from book 2 of *Paradise Lost*:

> O'er many a dark and dreary vale
> They pass'd, and many a region dolorous;
> O'er many a frozen, many a fiery Alp;
> Rock, caves, lakes, fens, bogs, dens and shades of death,
> A universe of death.

Regarding Milton's 'shades of death', Burke comments that this 'raises
a very great degree of the sublime', but then takes the argument
further, suggesting that 'this sublime is raised yet higher by what
follows, a *"universe of death"* '.[111] Conversely, death gets barely a
mention in Burke's discussions of beauty. The fear of death, it turns
out, is nothing less than the underlying dynamic of the sublime, the
yardstick against which other forms of fear and terror should be
measured. Looking for a way of capturing the terror of 'an entire life
of solitude' Burke's measure is death, 'since death itself is scarcely an
idea of more terror'.[112] Scipio and Cato are both virtuous characters,
'but we are more deeply affected by the violent death of the one . . .
than with the deserved triumphs and uninterrupted prosperity of the
other'.[113]

What is perhaps perplexing about Burke's arguments here is that if,
'politically' speaking, the dead are to be praised and revered for being
dead, then why is that, 'aesthetically' speaking, death is something to
be so feared? The real issue in linking the *Philosophical Enquiry* and
the *Reflections*, it seems, is not so much that Burke has moved from
championing the aesthetics of originality and individual experience to
championing authority and precedent, but that there is a tension
between a set of psychological and aesthetic assumptions about the
fear of death on the one hand, and a set of political and philosophical
demands for reverence for the dead on the other. Yet the tension is
resolved with Burke's notion of the sublime, and we are now in a
position to further see why the Revolution had to be understood as a
false sublime. For if death is the underlying dynamic of the sublime,
then the political position which comes closest to grasping the
significance of death is the one which can lay greatest claim to being a
form of politics centred on a proper understanding of the sublime and
thus, in a sense, sublime in itself. In other words, Burke's reverence for
the dead and his political articulation of a contract between those
living, those yet to be born and those already dead is a politics which
aspires to grasping the sublimity of the dead.

The only political position which can grasp this sublimity is one which
holds that society is eternal. If society is eternal, then the present itself is
a manifestation of eternal society. This is why the present must be
protected from the radicals and revolutionaries. We reform, says the
conservative, to preserve; and we seek to preserve the present. At the
heart of this idea is a politics of reconciliation. Reconciliation involves
accepting the present in its own right, to find a certain satisfaction in

the present – 'to delight in the present . . . is the *reconciliation* with actuality', says Hegel.[114] Reconciliation thus tends to postulate a situation supposedly prior to conflict or the outcome of some kind of 'resolution' to the conflict, marked by an ideological 'peace' and 'understanding' between otherwise contradictory forces or tendencies.[115] Reconciliation thus comes to figure as an essentially conservative mode of thought. That this is so can be seen in what is expected to be reconciled: individuals, nations and classes. Reconciliation of individuals with the present; which does not mean thinking that the present is perfect, but does mean accepting – reconciling ourselves with – its imperfections. (As conservatives have never stopped telling us, conservatism is the politics of imperfection.) Reconciliation of nations with (and despite) their very different traditions. And reconciliation of classes (which is very different to their abolition, a point to which I turn towards the end of the following chapter). But also being reconciled are generations – both past and future. What Burke is after, then, is nothing less than the *reconciliation* of the living and the dead. The revolutionaries, on this score, not only encourage division and antagonism between classes and groups, but also fail to register the eternal nature of society. And in so doing they are by definition antagonistic towards any reconciliation – especially of the generations and with the dead. For the revolutionaries 'mean to imitate some of their predecessors, who dragged the bodies of our antient sovereigns out of the quiet of their tombs'. They thus stand accused of 'gibbeting the carcass, or demolishing the tomb'.[116] In failing to show the proper respect for the dead, and thus for eternal society, the revolutionaries thus undermine the conservative project of reconciliation. Far from reconciliation, the revolutionaries want nothing less than the destruction of the dead – to drag bodies out of their tombs.

But this also takes us back to Burke's fear of the monstrous mob. The proletariat is both necessary to bourgeois order – who or what else is there to produce the wealth of nations? – and of course its greatest threat for that very reason. Thus the perennial problem for bourgeois politics is the political management of a proletariat. In Gothic terms, we might say that the proletariat is an entity which cannot be killed because the bourgeois order requires it to be living, but which as a *mob* cannot be assimilated into the current stable order – it is essentially disorderly. And as a *monster* it also cannot be properly assimilated into the glorious and 'safe' past. Why? Because as well as being an emblem of categorical anxiety, border concern and dis-ease, monsters are also *essentially undead*. And whatever the reason they keep coming back – as a warning, for revenge – they nonetheless keep coming back.[117] This claim and its relevance for understanding Burke will be fully sustained through Chapters 2 and 3 to follow. At this stage we might say that for the conservative the undead – that is, the monstrous multitude – are a problem because in *living* they cannot be reconciled into the image of the past, but as *dead* they refuse to lie down and be incorporated into history, reconciled to their fate. Baldick comments that 'to be a monster is to break the natural bonds of obligation towards friends and especially towards blood-relations'.[118] In Burkean terms we might say that to be a monster is to also break the bonds of obligation to the past and thus to the dead. Why this is a problem, however, will only become clear through the following two chapters.

2 • Marx: The Political Economy of the Dead

Towards the end of volume I of *Capital* Marx employs one of his usual dramatic and rhetorical devices: 'If money', he says, 'comes into the world with a congenital blood-stain on one cheek', then 'capital comes dripping from head to toe, from every pore, with blood and dirt'.[1] The comment is a reminder of the extent to which the theme of blood and horror runs through the pages of *Capital*. According to Stanley Hyman, there are in *Capital* two forms of horror. The first concerns the bloody legislation against vagabondage, describing the way that agricultural peoples were driven from their homes, turned into vagabonds and then 'whipped, branded, tortured by laws grotesquely terrible, into the discipline necessary for the wage system'. The second concerns the horrors experienced by people in the colonies, 'the extirpation, enslavement and entombment in mines of the aboriginal population, . . . the turning of Africa into a warren for the commercial hunting of black skins'.[2] But there is in fact a third form of horror: the constant sucking of the blood of the Western working class by the bourgeois class. This form is nothing less than the horror of a property-owning class which appears to be vampire-like in its desire and ability to suck the life out of the working class.

There has in recent years been a mass of literature on the spectre or ghostly in Marx's work, heavily influenced by or written in response to Jacques Derrida's *Specters of Marx*. What has not been discussed at anything like the same length in this context has been Marx's use of the vampire metaphor.[3] This is perhaps surprising, first, because of the obvious Gothic connection between the ghost and the vampire. Yet neither the one sustained attempt to 'theorize Gothic Marxism'[4] nor the treatment of Marx as a writer of 'Gothic fiction'[5] deal with the vampire. Other works which deal at greater length with Marx's vampire, such as Rob Latham's *Consuming Youth*, have ended up rerouting into political analyses of cultural formations and consumption.[6] Second, because what partly lies behind Derrida's interest in the spectral and the ghostly is the political importance of the dead. His work is about 'the state of mourning' – 'we will be speaking of nothing else'[7] – and our responsibility towards the dead.

As we shall see, this is also what lies behind the figure of the vampire. And third, because if anything the vampire metaphor plays a significant role in Marx's work, even more significant than the ghostly or spectral.

In this chapter I aim first to show the extent and significance of the vampire to Marx's work. This will allow me to consider, and reject, some possible interpretations of Marx's use of the vampire, before moving on to situate Marx's vampire in the very heart of his work: in the critique of political economy. This critique, I suggest, might be reconsidered as a critique of the political economy of the dead. This will allow me to broaden the discussion into a more general consideration of the political question of the dead in Marx's work.

Bloody capital

In the chapter on money in the *Grundrisse* Marx makes a comment in parentheses that runs as follows: 'To compare money with blood – the term circulation gave occasion for this – is about as correct as Menenius Agrippa's comparison between the patricians and the stomach.'[8] He seems to have here two targets. First, the organic and generally reactionary tradition in political thought which compared various 'parts' of society to various 'parts' of the body politic. And, second, the established analogy between capital and blood: the way both capital and blood are said to 'circulate', as he points out. This second target is important because its underlying assumption is that capital is somehow the 'lifeblood' of society. Adam Smith, for example, comments that 'blood, of which the circulation is stopt in some of the smaller vessels, easily disgorges itself into the greater, without occasioning any dangerous disorder; but, when it is stopt in any of the greater vessels, convulsions, apoplexy, or death, are the immediate and unavoidable consequences', and goes on to present the problems of monopoly in the colonies as 'a small stop in that great blood-vessel'.[9] This assumption that capital is the lifeblood of any economic system permeates both intellectual discourse and 'common sense' to this day. Not only is such an assumption ideological nonsense of the highest order, but Marx also thinks that it is the very opposite of the truth: far from being like blood, capital lives on the blood, and thus the lives, of the working class. Capital, in other words, is like a vampire.

Terrell Carver has pointed out that Marx uses the vampire metaphor three times in *Capital*.[10] Marx claims that 'capital is dead labour which, vampire-like, lives only by sucking living labour, and lives the more, the more labour it sucks'. He also comments that the prolongation of the working day into the night 'only slightly quenches the vampire thirst for the living blood of labour', because 'the vampire will not let go "while there remains a single muscle, sinew or drop of blood to be exploited" '.[11] If one also explores the text for comments that appear to derive from the vampire motif but fail to mention the vampire explicitly, then one finds a wealth of additional material. Capital 'sucks up the worker's value-creating power' and is 'dripping with blood'.[12] Lace-making institutions exploiting children are described as 'blood-sucking', while US capital is said to be financed by the 'capitalized blood of children'.[13] The appropriation of labour is described as the 'life-blood of capitalism', while the state is said to have here and there interposed 'as a barrier to the transformation of children's blood into capital'.[14]

If we take an even greater textual licence with *Capital* then the motif appears even more apparent. In the chapter on the working day Marx compares the development of the factory system with other historical forms of domination such as Athenian aristocracy, the Norman barons, the American slave-owners and the feudal *corvée*. In terms of the latter he notes that the legal mechanisms through which peasants performed forced labour on behalf of landowners could be stretched well beyond the stated number of stated days. The example he gives is of Wallachian peasants performing forced labour on behalf of the Wallachian boyars: 'For Moldavia the regulations are even stricter. "The 12 *corvée* days of the *Règlement organique*," cried a boyar, drunk with victory, "amount to 365 days in the year" '.[15] The source Marx cites for this is É. Regnault's *Histoire politique et sociale des principautés danubiennes* (1855). The 'Wallachian boyar' in this particular text turns out to be none other than Vlad the Impaler: Vlad Dracula.[16]

And if we extend the textual licence and situate *Capital* in other texts produced during its writing we find even more connections. In the *Grundrisse* capital is described as 'constantly sucking in living labour as its soul, vampire-like', or as 'sucking its living soul out of labour'.[17] In the 'Inaugural Address of the International Working Men's Association', given while in the middle of writing *Capital*, Marx describes British industry as 'vampire-like' which 'could but live by sucking blood, and children's blood too'.[18] That Marx uses the vampire in the context of the Inaugural Address is telling, since the internal wrangles within the association were enormous and Marx had to go to great lengths to keep all (or at least, most) sides happy. As Francis Wheen points out, the unanimous acceptance of the Address is a tribute to Marx's skill in judging precisely how far he could go in any direction. More telling, however, is that there are no revolutionary predictions, spectres or hobgoblins – yet the vampire remained.[19] And as Marx was putting the finishing touches to volume I of *Capital*, he wrote to Engels that a number of industries were being 'called to order' in a report by the Children's Employment Commission: 'the fellows who were to be called to order, among them the big metal manufacturers, and especially the vampires of "domestic industry", maintained a cowardly silence'.[20]

If one extends such a textual analysis to other major and minor works by Marx, it is clear that the vampire runs like a red thread through his work. In *The Class Struggles in France* he compares the National Assembly to a 'vampire that lived on the blood of the June insurgents'.[21] In *The Civil War in France* the agents of the French state, such as 'the notary, advocate, executor, and other judicial vampires', are all described as 'blood-suckers'.[22] In the *Eighteenth Brumaire* he comments that 'the bourgeois order . . . has become a vampire that sucks out its [the smallholding peasant's] blood and brains and throws them into the alchemists cauldron'.[23] The Wallachian boyar also makes a reappearance in both the *Eighteenth Brumaire* and *The Civil War in France*.[24]

The theme of the vampire had been present in the work of both Marx and Engels throughout the 1840s. In *The Condition of the Working Class in England*, the sociological observations of which filtered through into Marx's *Capital*, Engels had already toyed with the idea of the 'vampire property-holding class'.[25] In *The Holy Family* the two writers comment on a character of Eugene Sue's that 'he cannot possibly lead that kind of life without sucking the blood out of his little principality in Germany to the last drop like a vampire'.[26] In his unfinished journalism as 'The Correspondent from the Mosel' Marx had planned to write five sections, the fourth (and never written) of which was to be on 'The Vampires of the Mosel Region'.[27] And in an essay on the Prussian constitution of 1849 Marx comments on 'the Christian-Germanic sovereign and his accomplices, the whole host of lay-abouts, parasites and vampires sucking the blood of the people'.[28]

It is clear, then, that as a metaphor the vampire and its connotations play a key role in many of Marx's formulations. The question I wish to try and answer here is: why? More specifically, what does Marx mean when he describes capital as vampire-like?

One interpretation of Marx's use of the vampire metaphor might be to suggest that in and of itself the metaphor is merely another literary device employed by Marx. Like Burke, Marx is an incredibly imaginative writer. *Capital* in particular is chock-full of historical, philosophical and literary allusions, as many of the early reviews pointed out in commenting on the 'vigour of [Marx's] rhetoric' and the 'unusual liveliness' of his prose.[29] Robert Paul Wolff comments that:

> To read the opening chapters of *Capital* is to be plunged into an extraordinary literary world, quite unlike anything in the previous, or indeed subsequent, history of political economy. The text is rich in literary and historical allusions to the entire corpus of Western culture . . . Marx invokes religious images, Mephistophelean images, political images. He writes now mockingly and scornfully, now soberly and with proper professorial seriousness, now angrily and bitterly. He swings with baffling speed from the most abstruse metaphysical reflections to vividly sensual evocations of the sufferings and struggles of English workers against the oppression of their bosses. At one instant he is a polemicist, writing to the moment. At the next, he is a pedant, calling down authorities in six languages from twenty centuries to confirm his etymological tracings and analytical speculations.[30]

Likewise, Stanley Hyman comments that 'we get closer to the essential nature of *Capital* if we deal with it, not as science, social science, or exhortation, but as imaginative literature', while Marshall Berman builds his well-known reading of Marx's 'modernism' around the latter's 'luminous, incandescent prose' and 'brilliant images'.[31] On this view, one might be inclined to argue that Marx's references to the vampire are yet another literary tool in his entire armoury, part of what Marx himself described as the 'artistic' and 'literary' nature of his work, especially *Capital*.[32] In this sense it is sometimes suggested that '*Capital* is a dramatic poem, or possibly a dramatic epic' such that 'if we are not distracted by . . . its elaborate and energetic logic and its accumulation of evidence, we see that its concealed structure is mythical'. And as in all drama, the actors are often personifications of economic abstractions or, worse, they become other sorts of creatures – such as vampires.[33] Thus Marx's use of the vampire might well be merely one of his 'occult tropes', a technique used because of his recognition of 'how crucial it was to give an imaginative account of things'.[34] Moreover, we know that Marx enjoyed reading Gothic horror stories. And we know that the vampire was a popular literary form in the nineteenth century. While the best known novel of the genre, Bram Stoker's *Dracula*, was not published until 1897, after Marx's death, the vampire in general had had plenty of coverage prior to that. James Malcolm Rymer's *Varney the Vampire*, for example, serialized the year before the publication of *The Manifesto of the Communist Party*, stretched to 220 chapters over 868 pages. It may be, then, that 'more use-value and indeed profit can be derived from *Capital* if it is read as a . . . vast Gothic novel whose heroes are enslaved and consumed by the monster they created'.[35]

But simply describing Marx's use of the vampire as an imaginative rhetorical gesture is not quite enough. As we saw with Burke, literary style often has political or philosophical presuppositions. Wolff is therefore right to point out that 'Marx's literary style constitutes a deliberate attempt to find the philosophically appropriate language for expressing the ontological structure of the social world'.[36] Much as *Capital*, for example, may be read as a work of high literary art, its dominant metaphors and ironic structure serve a deliberate philosophical and political purpose. The choice of metaphor is thus philosophically and politically important: through it Marx aims to make a substantive point about the social world. Since the vampire is a parasite, Marx could have simply chosen the term 'parasite' or 'leech' or something similar; but he chose not to. So what is it about the vampire that encouraged Marx to use it so frequently?

It might be thought that the answer to this question could come from cultural studies, which has returned time and again to the meaning of the Gothic in general and the vampire in particular. Either through analyses of popular fiction, film and television, or through a wider focus on the culture of the Gothic, cultural studies has developed and sustained an interest in the vampire and its meanings. Space does not allow a full discussion of each of the variety of interpretations the vampire has within cultural studies, but the common feature is that they more or less all participate in what Chris Baldick and Robert Mighall call the 'anxiety model' of Gothic criticism.[37] Such anxiety is said to be generated by the vampire's alien features – its 'otherness' or 'difference' in the *lingua franca* of contemporary theory. Like the monster in general, the vampire is said to be the 'harbinger of category crisis', refusing easy categorization in the 'order of things', disrupting the borders of both nature and society. Donna Haraway, for example, writes that 'defined by their categorical ambiguity and troubling mobility, vampires do not rest easy (or easily) in the boxes labeled good and bad. Always transported and shifting, the vampire's native soil is more nutritious, and more *unheimlich*, than that.'[38] The vampire is in part a harbinger of category crisis because like the monster in general, s/he represents a form of difference.

Within cultural studies many writers have connected this 'difference' and/or 'otherness' with the scapegoat and thus oppressed and marginalized groups. Following the connection between the monster and the scapegoat drawn by René Girard,[39] the vampire has been interpreted as the figure of the Jew,[40] a transgressive sexuality either in general[41] or in a particular form such as the homosexual,[42] and travellers of all sorts. In particular, it has been argued that the vampire forms a cultural representation of the terrifying 'otherness' of female sexuality. Early vampires were often understood in terms of the *femme fatale* or dangerous woman, and cultural readings ever since have focused on the portrayal of a hungry and thus dangerous female sexuality in the culture of the vampire – the 'vamp' in other words.[43]

But there are serious problems in trying to use such analyses to make sense of what Marx is doing. For while it may be the case that the Gothic has always contained an intense, if displaced, engagement with political and social problems, in terms of cultural interpretations of the vampire the precise nature of the problems, the displacement and the engagement is so blurred and undefined that, rather than identifying the vampire with one particular group, an attempt is made to have it all ways by identifying the vampire with lots of groups. Judith Halberstam writes that Dracula 'can be read as aristocrat [and yet] a symbol of the masses; he is predator and yet feminine, he is consumer and producer, he is parasite and host, he is homosexual and heterosexual, he is even a lesbian'.[44] For Burton Hatlen, as a marauding and sexually perverse aristocrat, Dracula is a threat and yet, because of his smell and colour, he is representative of the working class. Thus the vampire 'represents both the repressed masses of workers and a decaying aristocracy'.[45] The point, it seems, is that rather than this or that other, the vampire is *all* other(s): 'otherness itself', as more than one cultural analysis has put it.[46] The vampire is a 'composite of otherness'[47] and thus a 'highly overdetermined threat'.[48] As Hatlen comments in a mode of argument aiming at developing a Freudian-

Marxist account of the vampire and yet typical of cultural studies of the vampire:

> Count Dracula represents the physically 'other': the 'dark' unconscious, the sexuality that Victorian England denied, more specifically a sado-masochistic sexuality that recognizes no limits and that no structured order can accept. He is also culturally 'other': a *revenant* from the ages of superstition when people believed that the communion wafer *was* the flesh of Christ. But more specifically of all he is the socially other: the embodiment of all the social forces that lurked just beyond the frontiers of Victorian middle class consciousness: the psychically repressed and the socially oppressed.[49]

On these grounds, the myriad and often contradictory interpretations of precisely which 'other' group the vampire is a metaphor for – the perverse heterosexual and yet gay/lesbian, the proletarian and yet aristocratic foreigner from within – appear perfectly reasonable, since 'it is "otherness" itself, not some particular social group, that the vampire represents; and, for the bourgeoisie, the modes of otherness are infinite'.[50]

This tendency to treat the vampire as a metaphor for the repressed, oppressed and outlawed has created a parallel tendency within cultural studies to treat the vampire as a subversive and thus liberating figure, on the rather simple (and simplistic) grounds that its very 'otherness' makes the vampire a threat to bourgeois order. As the oppressed, repressed and outlawed the vampire is simultaneously an 'antibourgeois' 'symbol of injustice'.[51] S/he thus 'threatens the tight, tidy world of upper middle class England'.[52] As such, the vampire's subversiveness is taken as read. Far from being undermined by what might appear to the uninitiated as essentially conflicting and thus mutually exclusive interpretations of the vampire – Is its meaning racial, sexual, political, social? What on earth does a lesbian male look like? Just what is an aristocratic symbol of the masses? – the purported subversiveness is said to be *enhanced* by these conflicts. This is why cultural studies of the vampire fit so neatly into Baldick and Mighall's 'anxiety model' account of Gothic criticism. As they explain, the model employs an account of

> culture and history premised on fear, experienced by . . . a caricature of a bourgeoisie trembling in their frock coats at each and every deviation from

a rigid, but largely mythical, stable middle-class consensus. Anything that deviates from this standard is hailed as 'subversive', with [the vampire] standing as the eternal principle of subversion – Otherness itself, to be fashioned according to the desires and agendas of the critic.[53]

Yet while such discussions may have an obvious appeal within, say, cultural analyses of film or popular literature, they do not really help us when it comes to understanding what Marx is doing when using the vampire. He is hardly using it as a gendered idea or in terms of transgressive sexuality; nor, *contra* Haraway's cheap but influential comment on 'Marx's . . . anti-Semitic vampire tropes',[54] can Marx's use of the vampire metaphor be explained according to the representation of the Jew – the vampire motif does not appear in his discussions of Judaism in 'On the Jewish Question'. And of the many points Marx tries to make about the social world, none of them can be read as a critique of 'otherness'; Marx was hardly an existential or postmodern cultural theorist *avant le lettre*.

An alternative way into the subject might be to read Marx's use of the vampire metaphor in terms of the kind of writers we know Marx was familiar with who had also at some point concerned themselves with the vampire. On this score Carver situates Marx's vampire metaphor in the longer history of interest in the vampire expressed by the eighteenth-century Enlightenment thinkers. He suggests that Marx's approach to the vampire 'was every bit as rationalist as one would expect, having its roots in the *philosophes* themselves'.[55] A fair amount of historical and literary evidence might be adduced for this claim. The eighteenth century was indeed a period of unprecedented interest in the vampire. The century saw a large number of 'vampire epidemics': in Istria (1672), East Prussia (1710, 1721, 1750), Hungary (1725–30), Austrian Serbia (1725–32), Silesia (1755), Wallachia (1756) and Russia (1772). The word 'vampyre' first entered the English language in the 1680s (not 1734 as the *OED* has it) and French in the 1690s (and became a household word after 1746). It was a familiar word in scholarly debate in Germany by the 1720s. Fourteen books appeared on the subject in Germany in 1732, and it has been estimated that forty treatises on vampirism were researched and published at German and French universities between 1728 and the early 1840s.[56] Unsurprisingly, then, the question of the vampire became an important issue for Enlightenment thinkers. As Christopher Frayling puts it, the age of reason was much perplexed by the question of vampirism.[57]

In general, the assumption of the *philosophes* was that since the vampire was beyond the bounds of possibility, the vampire itself was either a subject of no interest or, better still, a subject to be dismissed as a product of ignorant and unenlightened minds. Voltaire's entry for 'Vampires' in his *Dictionnaire philosophique* (1764) begins with a rhetorical and dismissive question: 'What! Is it in our eighteenth century that vampires exist? Is it after the reigns of Locke, Shaftesbury, Trenchard, and Collins? Is it under those of D'Alembert, Diderot, St. Lambert, and Duclos, that we believe in vampires?'[58] In the same vein, the two 'most eminent physicians' sent by Maria Theresa to ascertain the exact nature of the occurrences in Silesia in 1755 concluded that 'it was all the result of vain fears, superstitious beliefs, the dark, disturbed imagination, simplicity and ignorance of the people'.[59] In a slightly different vein, Rousseau concedes that in one sense vampires do indeed exist – in the minds of those who had attested to their existence – and that this existence is important because it raises questions concerning how one interprets the world and, more importantly, the kinds of authorities that verify such interpretations. In a letter to Christophe de Beaumont, the archbishop of Paris, Rousseau observes that 'if there is in the world an attested history, it is just that of vampires. Nothing is lacking; depositions, certificates of notables, surgeons, curés and magistrates. The proof in law is utterly complete. Yet with all this, who actually believes in vampires? Will we all be condemned for not believing in them?'[60] For Rousseau, vampires are 'miraculous' phenomena 'attested' to by all the major authorities, with the corollary that the same authorities will thus condemn us if we fail to accept the claims for the existence of vampires. In other words, vampire beliefs are evidence of the way the institutions of authority are legitimised by superstitious and unenlightened beliefs.

So one source of Marx's vampire metaphor may well have been the eighteenth-century Enlightenment and its main thinkers. But while the unprecedented eighteenth-century interest and Enlightenment concern with the vampire is likely to have influenced Marx – and is undoubtedly a more plausible explanation than the suggestion that Marx's use of the vampire is linked to his use of images drawn from the pre-capitalist world[61] – as an answer to the question as to why Marx is so interested by the vampire metaphor it is insufficient. Carver's suggestion that in using the vampire metaphor Marx was 'alluding to the arguments of the *philosophes*, Rousseau and Voltaire among others, that the true significance of . . . vampires and other popular superstitions was to bolster the sacred and secular authorities in society',[62] does not seem to be borne out by the citations from Marx given above. When Marx uses the vampire metaphor he seems far from ridiculing it as a superstitious belief. While he may not be suggesting the vampire really exists, he uses it as a metaphor to capture something very real indeed, namely a particular relation between human beings. It is true that Marx sometimes makes reference to institutions of authority when using the metaphor. As the examples cited earlier show, he refers to the French National Assembly as a vampire living off the blood of the June insurgents and other agents of the French state as 'blood-suckers' or 'judicial vampires'. But *pace* Rousseau, Marx is not suggesting that the vampire is *useful* to the authorities by bolstering their position of interpretive power. Rather, he is clearly suggesting that the authorities themselves are like vampires. Although Rousseau attempts to situate the vampire in the wider context of authority in society, his position is not quite the same as that of Marx. While it may be that 'Rousseau may have been attracted to the vampire image because it offered a vivid means of symbolising modes of mutual dependence in society which were not benign',[63] it is not at all clear that he is doing with the vampire image the same as Marx. His vision may have been of a 'master–slave dialectic, with teeth', as Frayling puts it, but it does not appear to have the same implications as Marx's.

Now, there is in some Enlightenment thought a little of Marx's sense. It can be found, for example, in Voltaire's entry on vampires in his *Dictionary*. Voltaire comments that 'in both these cities [Paris and London] there were stock-jobbers, brokers, and men of business, who sucked the blood of the people in broad daylight; but they were not dead, though corrupted. These true suckers lived not in cemeteries, but in very agreeable palaces', adding that 'the true vampires are the churchmen, who eat at the expense of both kings and people'.[64] Similar comments can be found in other eighteenth-century writings. In England in the 1730s *The Craftsman* presented Walpole and the past and present directors of the South Sea Company as vampires sucking the blood of their country.[65] Charles Forman, in his *Observations Upon the Revolution of 1688* (1741), compares merchants who bring money into the country with the 'Set of Men amongst us who have as great an Address in sending it out again to foreign countries without any Returns for it . . . These are the Vampires of the Publick, the Riflers of the Kingdom'.[66] And during the

1750s rumours of a blood-sucking monarch circulated throughout Paris, remaining part of radical-popular folklore until the revolution of 1789. Jacques-Nicolas Billaud-Varenne, for example, presenting a new organization of state and society to the Convention on 28 Brumaire Year II, comments on 'the authorities who were the perennial vampires of liberty'.[67] This perhaps gets us closer to what Marx is trying to do with the idea. And yet, as I shall now aim to show, it misses what is truly distinctive about Marx's position.

Living and dead labour

One standard interpretation of the vampire is to see him as representative of a feudal aristocrat. 'Vampires are always aristocrats', we are told.[68] Likewise, Chris Baldick writes that Dracula 'turns . . . towards an older kind of Gothic novel in which the bourgeoisie flirtatiously replays its victory over the baronial despot: Dracula is feudalism's death warmed up'.[69] In contrast to this view, however, is the far more common view which holds that the vampire is in fact more representative of capital and the bourgeois class than land and the aristocracy. This view is most closely associated with Franco Moretti's essay on the dialectic of fear. Situating his account in the context of Bram Stoker's *Dracula*, Moretti disregards the conventional account of the vampire as an aristocrat. Dracula lacks the aristocrat's conspicuous consumption in the form of food, clothing, stately homes, hunting, theatre-going and so on. Moreover, the count disregards the usual aristocratic practice of employing servants – he drives the carriage, cooks the meals, makes the beds and cleans the castle himself. Far from being representative of the aristocratic class, Dracula's desire for blood is read by Moretti as a metaphor for capital's desire for accumulation. The more he gets the stronger he becomes, and the weaker the living on whom he feeds become. A constant hunger for blood means he is never satisfied and thus always seeking new victims: 'Like capital, Dracula is impelled towards a continuous growth, an unlimited expansion of his domain: accumulation is inherent in his nature.' This vampire is thus 'capital that is not ashamed of itself'.[70]

Moretti's essay has been hugely influential in developing a reading of the vampire as capital and thus capital as vampire. Haraway comments that 'the vampire is . . . the marauding figure of unnaturally

breeding capital, which penetrates every whole being and sucks it dry
in the lusty production and vastly unequal accumulation of wealth',[71]
while Nicholas Rance notes that 'the Gothic metaphor . . . turns out to
be merely a projection of the ruling capitalist economy'.[72] Other
writers make the same connection. Gelder, for example, comments
that 'the representation of capital or the capitalist as vampire . . .
mobilised vampire fiction at this time, to produce a striking figure
defined by excess and unrestrained appetite',[73] and Halberstam
suggests that capitalism is rather Gothic in that 'like the vampire [it]
functions through many different, even contradictory, technologies'.[74]
As David Skal sums it up in his cultural history of horror: the vampire
is 'a sanguinary capitalist'.[75] It is with this reading that Marx
and cultural studies might appear to overlap. Rance's comments
concerning the vampire novel includes the idea that this is used in
precisely the same sense as in Marx, while Gelder's suggestion is that
'the representation of capital or the capitalist as vampire was, then,
common to *both Marx* and to popular fiction in the nineteenth
century'. Halberstam simply notes that Marx mentions the vampire a
couple of times to describe an economic system which is 'positively
Gothic'.[76] In general, then, what happens in cultural studies of the
vampire is that the link between the vampire and capital is drawn,
Marx then becomes an obvious reference point, his comments on the
vampire are noted and thus the link is reiterated. This of course has
the added advantage of strengthening the cultural reading of the
vampire's subversiveness – for what could be more subversive than
Marxism? Unperturbed by the fact that the vampire can hardly be a
subversive 'other' creating fears and anxieties for the bourgeois class if
it is simultaneously capital itself (and equally unperturbed by the
ahistoricism involved in taking themes from *Dracula* and reading them
back into Marx's work), cultural studies happily co-opts Marx into its
reading of the vampire.

   Yet this co-opting does not quite paint the full picture; in fact, it
omits precisely what is distinctive about Marx's position. Part of the
implication of my argument, therefore, is that Marx's use of the
metaphor is in fact far more sophisticated than that suggested by many
cultural analyses. For Marx is not just suggesting that capital and the
vampire are alike in constantly sucking the life out of their victims, but
is actually making suggestive comments about the connection between
capital and death, and the extent to which this connection is embodied
in the ongoing commodification of contemporary society. The

implication of this is that the approach to the vampire which simply says the vampire 'represents' capital, and that this is why Marx uses the metaphor, has missed the point, assimilating Marx's position to those of a thousand others and disregarding the originality of Marx's position. In so doing cultural studies offers us an incredibly impoverished reading of Marx's work. Marx becomes a cultural theorist l ike all the others, and the truly original dimension of his work, the dimension on which he aimed to be judged in the most scholarly as well as the most political terms, gets left behind.[77]

This distinctiveness, I suggest, can only be obtained by situating Marx's vampire metaphor in the context of his critique of political economy. More to the point, we need to situate the metaphor in the context of what can only be described as the political economy of the dead; or, better still, the political economy of the *undead*. It is worth recalling here that the two essential characteristics of vampires are that they are nourished by sucking the blood of the living, and that they are not quite dead: the vampire is a deceased person who nonetheless manages to continues to live by sucking the blood of the living – an *un*dead person who first visits the living and then draws the latter into death, being reanimated himself in the process.[78] It is this, I shall argue, that makes Marx's use of the vampire particularly apt. Making such a point draws us into another argument entirely – an argument concerning the place of the dead within Marx's and Marxist thought.

Early in the *Eighteenth Brumaire* Marx makes the following comment:

> the social revolution of the nineteenth century cannot draw its poetry from the past, but only from the future. It cannot begin with itself before it has stripped off all superstition about the past. Earlier revolutions required recollections of past world history in order to dull themselves to their own content. In order to arrive at its own content, the revolution of the nineteenth century must let the dead bury their dead.[79]

This comment is Marx's reminder that any revolutionary movement should not be weighed down with the past. But it also alerts us to the fact that the dead play a significant role in Marx's work,[80] and suggests that one way to understand the vampire motif is through the role of the dead in Marx's critique of political economy.

Fundamental to Marx's critique of political economy is his understanding of the dual character of both the commodity and labour. Marx was at pains to show that the dual nature of labour – as concrete and abstract labour – was a key component of his argument. 'I was the first person to point out and examine critically this twofold nature of the labour contained in commodities', he comments in chapter 1 of *Capital*, a point he reiterates in a letter to Engels in August 1867, in which he suggests that the presentation of the double nature of labour is one of 'the best points in my book'.[81] A better claim to originality might well lie in the distinction Marx draws between living and dead labour. Dismissing the view that capital is something distinct from labour – such as being a value-producing entity in its own right – Marx argues that capital is nothing but accumulated labour. His distinction is thus between accumulated labour and labour per se or, as he often puts it, accumulated labour versus 'living labour'. 'What is the growth of accumulated capital? Growth of the power of accumulated labour over living labour';[82] 'capital does not consist in accumulated labour serving living labour as a means for new production. It consists in living labour serving accumulated labour as a means for maintaining and multiplying the exchange value of the latter'.[83] But if the distinction is between accumulated and living labour, then it makes perfect sense to treat the former, capital, as 'dead labour'.[84] Marx had toyed with this idea in the 1844 *Manuscripts*, combining the idea of capital as 'stored-up labour' with the idea of 'dead capital' or 'dead mammon'.[85] However, by the fully fledged critique of political economy in *Capital* and the *Grundrisse*, capital had been thought through as dead labour as distinct from living labour, a distinction which then becomes a cornerstone of Marx's critique of political economy. 'Owing to its conversion into an automaton, the instrument of labour confronts the worker during the labour process in the shape of capital, dead labour, which dominates and soaks up living labour-power.'[86] Hence 'the rule of the capitalist over the worker is nothing but the rule of the independent conditions of labour over the worker . . . the rule of things over man, of dead labour over living'.[87]

But although capital may be dead labour, capital is also a highly active social agent: 'capital-in-process, creative capital, sucking its living soul out of labour'.[88] The trouble with dead labour is that under the rule of capital it refuses to stay dead: like the vampire, it returns to thrive off and control the living. Capital thus appears as dead labour turned into a form of life which in turn destroys the workers. Capital in this sense is both dead (labour) and living (power). It is an '*alien* being', a 'mechanical monster', or 'animated monster', a 'monstrous objective power'.[89] It is, in the language of nineteenth-century Gothic, undead. Moreover, as an undead being it appears to have the power of resurrecting and animating the dead. 'By incorporating living labour into their *lifeless* objectivity, the capitalist simultaneously transforms value, i.e. past labour in its objectified and *lifeless* form, into capital . . . an animated monster.'[90] This is a fundamental part of the topsy-turvy world of capital that Marx is at pains to illustrate. Inactive machinery is useless – dead – without the active force of living labour: 'Iron rusts; wood rots . . . Living labour must seize on these things [and] change them from merely possible into real and effective use-values.' In other words, labour must 'awaken them from the dead'.[91] But because of this the world of capital is a world in which 'living labour appears as a mere means to realize objectified, dead labour, to penetrate it with an animating soul while losing its own soul to it'.[92] The appropriation by the capitalist of the worker's productive powers is a means by which 'living labour makes instrument and material in the production process into the body of its soul and thereby resurrects them from the dead'.[93]

It is because of this that Marx makes a great deal out of the way that within mechanized factory production living labour is 'subsumed under the total process of the machinery itself, as itself only a link of the system, whose unit exists not in the living workers, but rather in the living (active) machinery, which confronts his individual, insignificant doings as a mighty organism'.[94] 'The objective conditions of labour [i.e. capital] assume an ever more colossal independence, represented by its very extent, opposite living labour, and that social wealth confronts labour in more portions as an alien and dominant power.'[95] Capital as 'dead' (that is, 'objectified', or 'accumulated') is thus nothing less than a social relation of domination and exploitation. But it is a relation of domination in which the product of labour comes to appear as a *living* and thus *alien* thing. 'The product of labour appears as an *alien property*, as a mode of existence confronting living labour as independent . . . the product of labour, objectified labour, has been endowed by living labour with a soul of its own, and establishes itself opposite living labour as an *alien power*.' Living labour 'repulses this realization from itself as an alien reality', and hence posits itself as a form of 'not-being' compared to the being of this alien power. But since this alien force is so powerful, labour posits itself 'as the being of its not-being'.[96]

It is this distinction between living labour and the dead labour embodied in capital on the one hand, and the fact of capital as a living exploitative and alien power on the other, that provides the initial aptness of the vampire image.[97] But once the aptness of Marx's image is recognized, a host of connected readings follow. Because the production of surplus value relies on living labour working on dead labour, the length of the working day is of crucial political importance. Marx had already pointed out in 'Wage labour and capital' that 'capital does not *live* only on labour. A lord, at once aristocratic and barbarous, it drags with it into the grave the corpses of its slaves, whole catacombs of workers who perish in the crises.'[98] In *Capital* this possibility of capital literally sucking the life out of the workers is fed into the paramount political question concerning the length of the working day. Capital, with its desire for endless and incessant accumulation, runs the risk of literally working the working class to death: 'By extending the working day, therefore, capitalist production . . . not only produces a deterioration of human labour-power by robbing it of its normal moral and physical conditions of development and activity, but also produces the premature exhaustion and death of this labour-power itself.'[99] Thus the struggle for legal limits on the working day is nothing less than a struggle through which workers can be saved 'from selling themselves and their families into slavery and death'.[100]

Given the political importance attached to the length of the working day, it is unsurprising to find that a close textual analysis of *Capital* reveals that the vampire motif is one of the central tropes around which the chapter on the working day is structured. Indeed, the three times that Marx uses the vampire metaphor explicitly in *Capital* all occur in the chapter on the working day. Marx opens the chapter describing capital as dead labour which 'vampire-like, lives only by sucking living labour', returns to the point mid-way through the chapter by commenting on the way the 'vampire thirst for the living blood of labour' prolongs the working day into the night, and ends the chapter quoting Engels on the unwillingness of the vampire to let go while there remains a muscle, sinew or drop of blood to be exploited. It is also in this chapter that the Wallachian boyar makes his appearance.

This argument also helps shed a little more light on the question of alienation from Marx's earlier work and the related 'mystery' of commodity fetishism. For the sake of brevity, we can identify two aspects of Marx's arguments concerning alienation. On the one hand, he identifies the effects of capitalist production on the worker. Under capitalism the 'realisation of labour appears as *loss of realisation* for the workers; objectification as *loss of the object and bondage to it*, and appropriation as *estrangement, as alienation*'.[101] In such a system human beings are alienated from the activity of labour, the product and from other human beings and thereby also from themselves. This argument relies in part on Marx's related argument concerning the sensuous creature. In damaging human beings capital damages them as sensuous creatures – feeling, experiencing, sensing creatures. 'To be *sensuous*, that is, to be really existing, means to be an object of sense, to be a *sensuous* object, and thus to have sensuous objects outside oneself – objects of one's sensuousness. To be sensuous is to *suffer*.'[102] At the same time, 'Man as an objective, sensuous being is therefore a *suffering* being – and because he feels that he suffers, a *passionate* being. Passion is the essential power energetically bent on its object.' Passion is thus central to man's species-being.[103]

Marx here reverses Max Stirner's comments on sensuousness. Marx cites Stirner as conceiving of sensuousness as a vampire: 'sensuousness, like a vampire, sucks all the marrow and blood from the life of man'.[104] But for Marx the reverse is true: sensuousness is the foundation of our species-being; it is the vampire-like capital that is the death of true sensuousness. Thus only with the supersession of private property will human sensuousness be able to come into its own. 'The abolition of private property is therefore the complete *emancipation* of all human senses and qualities, but it is this emancipation precisely because these senses and attributes have become, subjectively and objectively, *human*.'[105] Only under communism will the human senses be able to be realized in the fullest sense, and man once more be able to *feel* like a genuinely *living* creature, as opposed to one ruled by the dead (capital). Only vampires (and necrophiliacs[106]) find anything sensuous in the dead.

On the other hand, Marx's argument in the 1840s also concerns the capitalist and the role of capital. 'The less you eat, drink, buy books, go to the theatre, go dancing, go drinking, think, love, theorize, sing, paint, fence, etc., the more you *save* and the greater will become that treasure which neither moths nor maggots can consume – your *capital*.'[107] Thus although sensuous powers are alienated under the rule of capital, the capitalist is able to recuperate the estranged sensuality through the power of capital itself:

> Everything which the political economist takes from you in terms of life and humanity, he restores to you in the form of *money* and *wealth*, and everything which you are unable to do, your money can do for you: it can

eat, drink, go dancing, go to the theatre, it can appropriate art, learning, historical curiosities, political power, it can travel, it is *capable* of doing all these things for you.[108]

As Terry Eagleton points out, capital here becomes a phantasmal body, a monster which stalks abroad while its master sleeps, consuming the pleasures the master forgoes – an image of the living dead.[109]

This argument in Marx's 'early works' becomes transformed in *Capital* into an account of commodity fetishism. While many writers have highlighted the 'metaphysical subtleties and theological niceties' that run through Marx's discussion in the section on the fetishism of the commodity and its secret, and have consistently pointed to the 'magical', 'spectral' and 'spiritual' dimensions to his argument, what is relevant here is the fact that the fetish in question concerns something Marx is describing as dead. Because capital is dead labour, the desire to live one's life through commodities is the desire to live one's life through the dead. What Marx is doing here is identifying nothing less than the '*necromancy* that surrounds the products of labour' (a necromancy that 'vanishes as soon as we come to other forms of production').[110] The 'horror' of fetishism is of course that it conjures up 'fantastic' – because 'transcendent' and 'mysterious' – beings.[111] But the horror also lies in the fact that these beings are conjured up out of the dead; the circulation of commodities thus becomes the autonomous movement of the undead. On this basis we might say that the 'secret' of commodity fetishism is that it allows the commodity fetish to *partake of the realm of the dead*. The trick of fetishism is that it is the inorganic realm of the dead which nonetheless makes the dead appear alive.[112] The vampire metaphor is thus particularly apt in this context for the metaphor is in part about the autonomous movement of the dead and the resulting subjugation and domination of the living.[113] The vampire, like the commodity, is dead and yet not dead – 'undead' – in the sense that they are dead persons/things who/which manage to live thanks to the sensuousness of the living. In being brought back to life in this way the vampire/ commodity comes to rule through a powerful dialectic of fear and desire.

It is clear, then, that when he uses the vampire metaphor Marx was indeed employing a rhetorical literary device, one gleaned not from 'classic literature' as many of his allusions are, nor from any of the 'great thinkers' he so often refers to either directly or elliptically, but one which plays on one of the many popular if irrational beliefs. But this was not *simply* a rhetorical device, for Marx uses it to illustrate one of the central dynamics of capitalist production – the distinction between living and dead labour, a distinction which picks up on a more general theme in his work: the desire to create a society founded on the *living* of full and creative lives rather than one founded on the *rule of the dead*. Writing for readers reared on and steeped in the central motifs of popular literature, Marx thus invoked one of its most powerful metaphors not only to force upon his readers a sense of the appalling nature of capital, namely its affinity with death, but to also then suggest that communism would consist of liberation of living labour (that is, sensuous human beings) from the rule of dead labour (that is, capital).

Redemption; or must we let the dead bury their dead?

There is however more to be said about the dead, beyond the question of the vampire. For Marx's interest in the dead goes well beyond the idea of capital as dead labour sucking the life out of the working class. In fact, following this argument through will take us to the heart of Marxism and to a central tension in revolutionary politics. It will also allow us simultaneously to return briefly to the question of conservatism and open the way for the discussion of fascism in the following chapter.

It was noted earlier that in the *Eighteenth Brumaire* Marx comments that the social revolution of the nineteenth century cannot draw its poetry from the past, but only from the future, and that such a revolution cannot begin before it has stripped off all superstition about the past. The passage cited ends with Marx's comment that 'in order to arrive at its own content, the revolution of the nineteenth century must let the dead bury their dead'. This phrase might appear to be a throwaway line – one more rhetorical gesture – but it is a phrase Marx was actually quite fond of repeating. When a decade earlier Ruge had written to Marx despairing of the lack of revolutionary movement in 1843, Marx replied that 'your letter, my dear friend, is a fine elegy, a funeral song, that takes one's breath away; but there is absolutely nothing political about it'. And he adds:

Nevertheless, you have infected me, your theme is still not exhausted, I want to add the finale, and when everything is at an end, give me your hand, so that we may begin again from the beginning. Let the dead bury their dead and mourn them. On the other hand, it is enviable to be the first to enter the new life alive; that is to be our lot.[114]

He repeats the point elliptically in his attack on Stirner in the *The German Ideology*[115] and elsewhere in the context of the aggressive policies of the capitalist class:

> They [the economists] only assert that new means of employment will open up for *other component sections of the working class*, for instance, for the portion of the young generation of workers that was ready to enter the branch of industry which has gone under. That is, of course, a great consolation for the disinherited workers. The capitalist gentlemen will never want for fresh exploitable flesh and blood, and will let the dead bury their dead.[116]

So we know Marx was fond of the phrase. But what on earth does it mean?[117]

Marx adopts the phrase from the Gospel of Matthew: 'Jesus said to him, "Follow me, and leave the dead to bury their own dead" ' (8: 22). Jesus makes the comment to a disciple who asks for time to be able to bury his father. The suggestion seems to be that the burying of the (physical) dead should be left to those who are spiritually dead. Jesus's radicalism here lies in his break with contemporary mores concerning the dead, seeming to suggest that a failure to make a break with the past (in the form of the physically dead) was tantamount to the spiritual death of the movement. The movement itself overrode obligations to the past. The point for Marx would seem to lie in the implication that this new *political* movement should not be burdened with the past. Humanity must learn to part with its past, as he puts it in his early critique of Hegel.[118]

Marx's use of the phrase seems to pick up on his sense of the danger for the communist movement of succumbing to the weight of the present and thus the weight of the past, a danger symbolized by the control the dead seem to have over the living. He comments in the preface to the first edition of *Capital* that 'we suffer not only from the living, but from the dead. *Le mort saisit le vif!*' ('The living are in the grip of the dead!') And as he puts it elsewhere, 'the tradition of all the dead generations weighs like a nightmare on the brain of the living'. Engels repeats this as one of Marx's insights.[119] The present – or, given the shifting temporality of modernity, at least the *nineteenth century* present – thus *suffers under the weight of the dead*. The extent of this weight or suffering can be seen in the fact that many revolutionary struggles have been understood in terms gleaned from the past: 'It is generally the fate of completely new historical creations to be mistaken for the counterpart of older and even defunct forms of social life.' Thus the Paris Commune of 1871 was 'mistaken for a reproduction of the medieval communes' or 'mistaken for an exaggerated form of the ancient struggle against over-centralization'.[120] In many cases this is because the revolutionaries themselves made the mistake, and continue to make the mistake, of turning to the dead, to past generations, in order to find their meaning and legitimacy.

> Just when they seem engaged in revolutionising themselves and things, in creating something that has never yet existed, precisely in such periods of revolutionary crisis they anxiously conjure up the spirits of the past to their service and borrow from them names, battle-cries and costumes in order to present the new scene of world history in this time-honoured disguise and this borrowed language.

Thus:

> Luther donned the mask of the Apostle Paul, the revolution of 1789 to 1814 draped itself alternately as the Roman Republic and the Roman Empire, and the revolution of 1848 knew nothing better to do than to parody, now 1789, now the revolutionary tradition of 1793 to 1795 . . . Camille Desmoulins, Danton, Robespierre, Saint-Just, Napoleon, the heroes as well as the parties and the masses of the old French Revolution, performed the task of their time in Roman costume and with Roman phrases.[121]

This is what Marx calls 'world-historical necromancy':

> the resurrection of the dead in those revolutions served the purpose of glorifying the new struggles, not of parodying the old; of magnifying the given task in imagination, not of fleeing from its solution in reality; of finding once more the spirit of revolution, not of making its ghost walk again.[122]

In contrast, the communist movement as envisaged by Marx and Engels is a movement for a world 'coming into being';[123] it creates its poetry from the future. Driven by what Peter Osborne describes as a *historical futurity*[124] the proletariat should not, in this view, be burdened by the past; it therefore must, in its creation of a new future, leave behind previous generations. Now, this futurity is somewhat dependent on what G. A. Cohen has called the obstetric motif in Marx's work.[125] Marx points out several times that the present is *pregnant* with possibility, such that the new society will *emerge from the womb* of the present. If 'force is the midwife of every old society', he comments in *Capital*, then every old society must be thought of as 'pregnant with a new one'.[126] Or: 'In our days, everything seems pregnant with its contrary'. Because communism 'will be the product that the present time bears in its womb', what we are dealing with is a society 'not as it has *developed* on its own foundations, but on the contrary, just as it *emerges* from capitalist society, which is thus in every respect, economically, morally and intellectually, still stamped with the birthmarks of the old society from whose womb it emerges'. The role of the communist movement is to 'shorten and lessen the birth-pangs' of the new society and 'set free the elements of the new society with which old collapsing bourgeois society itself is pregnant'. In contrast to the system of capital in which labour appears 'as a power springing forth from its own womb', communism will be a society which realizes 'the possibilities resting in living labour's own womb'. Bourgeois society thus carries communism within its womb. 'The longer the time that events allow to thinking humanity for taking stock of its position, and to suffering mankind for mobilising its forces, the more perfect on entering the world will be the product that the present time bears in its womb.'[127] To be a communist, then, is to be focused on the birth of the new rather than the death of the old – to act as midwife to the new society.

The combination of Marx and Engels's critique of previous revolutionary movements, the historical futurity implicit in the communist project and the clear desire to identify the present as a society pregnant with the possibility of communism, becomes central to the distinction drawn between the communism of the *Manifesto* and other forms of communism or socialism. In the section on 'Socialist and communist literature' Marx and Engels identify three forms of socialism:[128] first, reactionary socialism, and its three subforms: feudal socialism, petty-bourgeois socialism and German, or 'true', socialism; second, conservative, or bourgeois, socialism; and third, critical-utopian socialism and communism. What is partly at stake in the account of these three varieties is the question of what we might now call class alignment: feudal socialism joins forces with classes for which feudalism was most suited, namely the landed aristocracy; German or 'true' socialism tends to obliterate theoretically the question of class in its concern for 'Human Nature' or 'Man' and thus serves the class of philistines, the petty-bourgeoisie; conservative socialism aims at the maintenance of existing property relations minus its revolutionary element – that is, a bourgeoisie without a proletariat; the Utopian socialists appeal to society at large, with the consequence that they aim to stand apart from class struggle – the proletariat are merely seen as 'the most suffering class', not the class to be politically supported and organized. This dimension of the critique of socialist and communist literature in the *Manifesto* is well-known, being the basis of all sorts of clashes and denunciations in the First International and after. But what is also at stake in this discussion, and more relevant to the argument here, is a politics of time.

The defining characteristic of reactionary socialism is its desire to restore past social forms. Feudal socialism is a 'half echo of the past': it holds up past forms of exploitation as somehow better than present. Its petty-bourgeois version, for example, seeks to reinvigorate the corporate guilds as the basis for manufacture and therefore aims at 'restoring the old means of production and exchange, and with them the old property relations, and the old society'. In contrast to the reactionary forms of socialism, conservative socialism aims more at the maintenance of existing property relations but without the revolutionary potential within them. Rather than propose a radical rejection of modern conditions on the basis of a reactionary return to feudal or semi-feudal social structures, conservative socialism prefers to contemplate the possibility of 'the existing state of society minus its revolutionary and disintegrating elements'. Conservative socialism thus aims to maintain the bourgeois status quo, albeit with piecemeal reforms.

So, in contrast to the historical futurity of communism, other forms of socialism or communism are either backward-looking phenomena – 'for they try to roll back the wheels of history' – or merely aim at preserving the status quo. Against these, Marx and Engels set communism, as the only doctrine with a vision of a *future* transformation of the social conditions of bourgeois society into communist forms of property ownership. And while the critical-utopians base their socialism and communism on the future, they do so on the basis of 'fantastic pictures of future society' combined with a rejection of all political, and especially revolutionary, action. The point is thus that communism is a movement driven by the image of the *future*, and not the past, and founded on the *revolutionary movement of the proletariat*.

To reiterate: communism would appear to be a revolutionary movement for the future and should do all it can to avoid being weighed down by the past. In accepting communism as a movement aiming for the *birth* of a new society we seem obliged to accept the *thoroughness* of history in carrying old forms to the grave: 'Why this course of history? So that humanity should part with its past *cheerfully*. This *cheerful* historical destiny is what we vindicate.'[129] Reach for the future, and reach for it cheerfully; let the new society be born. Let the dead bury their dead.

Now, if nothing else, this argument has the virtue of consistency. If communism as conceived by Marx is driven by the birth of the future society, then it is perfectly consistent to suggest that we must let the dead bury their dead. It therefore appears quite conceivable that Marx saw the solidarity of a liberated mankind simply in terms of a principle of harmony amongst future generations, a view in which exploited predecessors and enslaved contemporaries are reduced to the status of nonentities or dead wood in the evolution of mankind and whose existence had best be forgotten. According to this view, held by many and assumed to be held by Marx, the human species actualizes itself when it overcomes the debilitating ballast of remembrance; that is, when it *forgets* its historical genesis. Marxism thus becomes a politics designed as the emancipation from remembrance, and communism a movement so driven by the prospects of the future that it sees emancipated mankind leaving behind as 'prehistory' all previous struggles and past sufferings. On this view the dead are to be abandoned to the past, and the past is to be abandoned as dead. What else could be intended by Marx when he comments in the *Manifesto* that while 'in bourgeois society . . . the past dominates the present', under communism 'the present dominates the past'?[130] The revolutions of the nineteenth century and onwards must turn away from the past. As Derrida puts it, such revolutions 'must no longer even do that mourning work in the course of which the living maintain the dead, play dead, busy themselves with the dead, let themselves be entertained and occupied and *played or tricked* by the dead, speak *them* and speak *to them*, bear their name and hold forth in their language'.[131] The beauty of this interpretation, what instinctively makes it appear to work, is that it appears to have a wonderful symmetry vis-à-vis Burke. Where Burke appears to *sanctify* the dead under the banner of tradition, Marx appears to wish to *abandon* dead generations under the banner of revolution. Marxism and conservatism would thus appear diametrically opposed, as in many ways they should be.

And yet there is something that is not quite right about this interpretation. On one level the argument has a certain obviousness – at the most basic of levels communism must be about the future, in a way that conservatism must be about the past and tradition. But there is a sense in which the purported asymmetry between Marxism and conservatism simply comes too easy. More to the point, there is an important sense in which the argument simply omits much that is important to Marxism.

Marx reiterates time and again that human beings make their own history, but they do not do so under circumstances of their own choosing. They build it out of the world from which they have emerged. In other words, human beings *inherit from the dead* the circumstances in which they find themselves, an inheritance formed not least out of the struggles of dead generations. Thus as much as one might wish that we can leave the dead to bury their dead, the tradition of dead generations nonetheless still *weighs like a nightmare on the brain of the living*. The struggle for the future is therefore 'not a question of drawing a great mental dividing line between past and present'. There is no absolute distinction between today and yesterday. Rather, it is a question of '*realising* the thoughts of the past'. In other words, in the project of communism mankind 'is not beginning a *new* work' in the way that the obstetric motif would seem to suggest, 'but is consciously *carrying into effect its old work*'.[132]

Moreover, Marx's powerful arguments concerning the development of feudalism into capitalism convey the sense of injustice he obviously perceives in this historic transformation, captured in the three types of horror with which we opened this chapter: the bloody processes and laws through which agricultural peoples were forced from their homes, turned into vagabonds and then whipped, branded and tortured into the discipline necessary for the wage system; the horrors, extirpation and enslavement experienced in the colonies through which whole continents were turned into warrens for the commercial hunting of black skins; and, of course, the constant sucking of the blood of the Western working class by the bourgeois class, a process in which the workers are often worked literally to death. Marx clearly believes that communism is nothing if it fails to build on the sense of injustice experienced by those alive at the fate of their dead. From remembrance of those who died struggling against capital (or for merely trying to live in ways not determined by capital) to the struggle for justice for those killed in the corporate slaughterhouse (called 'industrial accidents' in bourgeois ideology); from the thousands killed by imperialist and colonial ventures to the millions starved to death in various exercises of the free market; from those killed in the fight against fascism to the struggle for retribution against deaths 'in police custody'; from the campaign against 'dead peasants' insurance in the US to the fight for a workers memorial day in the UK: the list is endless. They are all part of the blood-drenched history which animates contemporary struggles of the living and which either implicitly or explicitly echo Adorno's suggestion, noted earlier, that one of the basic human rights possessed by those who pick up the tab for the progress of civilization is the right to be remembered. It is a sense of the struggles of the past that often drives a movement to struggle for a certain future; the struggle for the future would thus surely be seriously lost if it gave up the struggle for justice for the dead.

Taken together these ideas point towards the fact that the revolutionary tendency of the proletariat does not come from nowhere, but emerges from historical conditions which have themselves been shaped by struggle. It is partly this that drove Marx into spending more time thinking and writing about the past than the future – after all, is not Marx constantly reproached with having written ten to twenty volumes about past and contemporary economics while producing barely ten pages on the future?[133] When Marx talks about the past in these ways he seems to be making a point very different to the idea that we must abandon the dead to their fate. Rather, he seems to be articulating a position which suggests that there exists a *unity of the oppressed*, a unity rooted in the historical emergence and continued existence of class society. This unity, one might suppose, suggests a solidarity, albeit undefined, between the living and the dead. Derrida picks up on this suggestion in his stress on the political importance of mourning:

> No justice . . . seems possible or thinkable without the principle of some *responsibility*, beyond all living present, within that which disjoins the living present, before the ghosts of those who are not yet born or who are already dead, be they victims of wars, political or other kinds of exterminations,

victims of the oppressions of capitalist imperialism or any of the forms of totalitarianism.[134]

But rather than follow Derrida into the realm of mourning and spectres I will instead take up Lenhardt's suggestion that this responsibility or sense of unity with dead generations should be thought of as an *anamnestic solidarity*, a form of solidarity expressed through the process of remembrance and which finds no better expression than in Marx's suggestion that the modern proletariat is de facto the heir of legions of exploited workers and slaves of the past.[135] Historical materialism would be politically weakened if it involved forgetting that communism will be built on the bodies and memory of those who have struggled and died in the past: 'only the conscious horror of destruction creates the correct relationship with the dead: unity with them because we, like them, are the victims of the same condition and the same disappointed hope'.[136] I suggest that such an anamnestic solidarity can be developed through the category of redemption, an idea which I will then contrast to the conservative notion of reconciliation and, in Chapter 3, the fascist concept of resurrection.

Marx played with the idea of redemption in his early work, where he suggests that the proletariat 'can redeem itself only through the *total redemption of humanity*'.[137] But he never developed this at any length. To do so, I shall turn to the Marxist who was most sensitive to the idea of redemption: Walter Benjamin. In his theses 'On the Concept of History' Benjamin suggests that 'the idea of happiness is indissolubly bound up with the idea of redemption'. The same applies to the idea of the past, and thus history. 'The past carries with it a secret index by which it is referred to redemption . . . There is a secret agreement between past generations and the present one.'[138] To grasp this secret – to 'articulate the past historically' – means neither trying to recognize it 'the way it really was' nor to attempt any kind of 'total recall', both of which feature as the myth of historicism (or at least, Benjamin's understanding of historicism, which in conflating both objectivism and progressivism in history has a peculiarity of its own). For Benjamin, the historicist attempt to narrate things 'as they really were' is in fact a form of forgetting: ' "if you want to relive an epoch, forget that you know what has come after it". That is the secret Magna Charta for the presentation of history by the Historical School.'[139] Forget, that is, that what are now called 'cultural treasures' have an origin which cannot truly be contemplated without horror; forget that the documents of civilization are at the same time documents of barbarism.[140]

In contrast to historicism, history for Benjamin 'is the subject of a construction whose site is not homogeneous, empty time, but time filled full by now-time (*Jetztzeit*)'. Not only is the 'now' thus a *historical* present but, conversely, the historical is filled by the presence of the now. This gives rise to a reading of the French Revolutionary use of ancient motifs very different to that suggested by Marx in the *Eighteenth Brumaire* or the *Manifesto*. In contrast to Marx's suggestion that in performing the Revolution in Roman costume and with Roman phrases the French were engaged in world-historical necromancy, Benjamin suggests that 'to Robespierre ancient Rome was a past charged with now-time, a past which he blasted out of the continuum of history. The French Revolution viewed itself as Rome reincarnate. It cited ancient Rome exactly the way fashion cites a bygone mode of dress'.[141] For Benjamin, the French revolutionaries were doing something more profound than Marx was willing to make allowances for: they were working with an image of the past which captured their own concerns in the now; they at least recognized that historical tradition is part of the terrain of the class struggle.

Benjamin thus rejects any concept of history as an uninterrupted series past–present–future in favour of a concept of history in which past and present are intermingled. His 'now-time' expands the historical content of the present to infinity.[142] This concept of history is thought to be in keeping with the 'tradition of the oppressed', a tradition under threat from the commitment to 'progress' on the part of both historicism and social democracy.

The subject of historical knowledge is the struggling, oppressed class itself. Marx presents it as the last enslaved class – the avenger that completes the task of liberation in the name of generations of the downtrodden. This conviction, which had a brief resurgence in the Spartacus League, has always been objectionable to Social Democrats. Within three decades they managed to erase the name of Blanqui almost entirely, though at the sound of that name the preceding century had quaked. The Social Democrats preferred to cast the working class in the role of a redeemer of *future* generations, in this way cutting the sinews of its greatest strength. This indoctrination made the working class forget both its hatred and its spirit of sacrifice, for both are nourished by the image of enslaved ancestors rather than by the ideal of liberated grandchildren.[143]

The greatest strength of the movement thus lies in the repository of historical knowledge held by the oppressed class – it is only 'the tradition of the oppressed', for example, which teaches us that the state of emergency in which we live is not the exception but the rule.[144] Our concept of history both requires and leads us to make a choice. The same threat hangs over both the content of the tradition and those who seek to maintain it: the danger of becoming a tool of the ruling class. The nature of this threat stands out most clearly if one asks with whom one empathizes: for the adherents of historicism it is the victors; for the historical materialist it is the enslaved ancestors.

Underlying Benjamin's opposition to historicism, and his insistence that historical materialism needs to make history explode with the images of enslaved ancestors, is his belief that if historical materialism fails to supply such an experience of the past, the dead will not be safe. 'The only historian capable of fanning the spark of hope in the past is the one who is firmly convinced that *even the dead* will not be safe from the enemy if he is victorious.'[145] This is the 'unique experience with the past' supplied by historical materialism. But the problem is that the enemy – fascism – has not ceased to be victorious. Benjamin is concerned not only that Marxism has failed to be sufficiently nourished or mobilized by the image of enslaved ancestors, but that should this failing continue then the same enslaved ancestors will themselves not be safe from the enemy. Historical materialism thus needs to engage in 'a revolutionary chance in the fight *for* the oppressed past'.[146] Our task is nothing less than to protect the dead. To 'let the dead bury their dead' would therefore not only fail to fan the spark of hope embodied in the images of enslaved ancestors, it would be politically disastrous. The dead will not be safe, and neither will we.

This argument is bound up with Benjamin's concept of redemption: 'Only a redeemed mankind receives the fullness of its past.'[147] A combination of a secret agreement between generations and the image of enslaved ancestors on the one hand, and a sustained class hatred on the other (a hatred fuelled by the depth of historical knowledge), is the basis of redemption, in which liberation is completed in the name of oppressed ancestors. This is the foundation of Benjamin's image of the angel of history in the ninth thesis.

> There is a picture by Klee called *Angelus Novus*. It shows an angel who seems about to move away from something he stares at. His eyes are wide, his mouth is open, his wings are spread. This is how the angel of history

must look. His face is turned toward the past. Where a chain of events appears before *us, he* sees one single catastrophe, which keeps piling wreckage upon wreckage and hurls it at his feet. The angel would like to stay, awaken the dead, and make whole what has been smashed.[148]

Many commentators have interpreted this image as yet another sign of the messianic dimension of Benjamin's work, but there is nothing messianic about the ninth thesis – historical wakening is, for Benjamin, one of the foundation stones of dialectical thinking.[149] The angel stands for the 'true' historian, that is, the historical materialist, who sees those lying prostrate, the horror which has produced the cultural treasures, the sky-high wreckage and pile of debris, and senses that even the dead will not be safe from the enemy. Far from being a Messiah come to save us, the angel in question would like to stay and do nothing less than *awaken the dead.* Now, for obvious reasons it could only be a wish that one could wake the dead (and as we shall see, this *sounds* dangerously like the fascist concept of resurrection). But the motivation behind Benjamin's suggestion is the idea that without the preservation of this wish as a wish they would die a second time – at the hands of the enemy. And this task of protecting the dead is not assigned to a redeemer who intervenes from outside history; rather, it is *our task.*[150]

For Benjamin, then, 'historical materialism sees the work of the past as still uncompleted'.[151] This comment comes in an essay on Edmund Fuchs published three years prior to the theses on the concept of history. Benjamin had sent the essay to Horkheimer for publication in the *Zeitschrift für Sozialforschung.* In a letter to Benjamin from March 1937 Horkheimer offers a very different conception of the image of enslaved ancestors in historical materialism. He comments that 'past injustice has occurred and is completed. The slain are really slain . . . Perhaps, with regard to incompleteness, there is a difference between the positive and the negative, so that only the injustice, the horror, the sufferings of the past are irreparable.'[152] This is an integral part of the pessimism that Horkheimer readily (and proudly?) concedes is at the heart of critical theory, as he makes clear in published essays: 'perfect justice' can never become a reality, because 'even if a better society develops and eliminates the present disorder, there will be no compensation for the wretchedness of past ages and no end to the distress in nature'.[153] Similarly, 'past injustice will never be made up; the suffering of past generations receives no compensation'.[154] While articulating a position that may appear closer to that initially identified with Marx's, Horkheimer here misses the intention and distinctiveness of Benjamin's argument. After all, Benjamin was hardly averse to a little pessimism himself – 'pessimism all along the line. Absolutely.'[155] In reporting on this exchange with Horkheimer in one of the notebooks for the 'Arcades Project', Benjamin comments that historical materialism is here concerned less with the 'determined facts' and more with the politics of remembrance. Benjamin thus senses that remembrance and redemption could be the cornerstones of a historical materialist approach. But when he writes that every image of the past that is not recognized by the present as one of its own concerns threatens to disappear irretrievably, Benjamin is not arguing for some kind of total recall or the recovery of the past 'the way it really was'; nor is he succumbing to 'the cult of remembrance of dead or absent loved ones', which manifests itself in, for example, bourgeois portraiture or their 'enshrinement as heritage'.[156] Rather, Benjamin is 'pointing to a politics of memory for which the character of the present, and hence the future, is determined by its relations to a series of specific pasts ("enslaved ancestors", for example, as opposed to triumphs of nation)'.[157] One of the underlying principles of his work was thus to develop a materialist concept of history founded on 'images in the collective consciousness in which the new is permeated with the old', in which 'the entire past is brought into the present', and in which the present recognizes itself as intimated in the image of the past – a cultural-historical dialectic which Benjamin liked to describe as apocatastasis, a term derived from the Jewish apocalyptic, Stoic and Neoplatonic–Gnostic traditions meaning the 'restoration of all things'.[158] The relations to the past contained within the notion of restoration are driven by the secret agreement between past generations and the present one. 'Like every generation that preceded us, we have been endowed with a *weak* Messianic power, a power on which the past has a claim.'[159] Such a 'claim' would appear to be a political right that past generations have vis-à-vis the power of redemption possessed by the living. Memory thus becomes the secret of redemption.[160]

But wait a minute. Is all this stuff about the past not beginning to sound a little, well, conservative? In a critical profile of Benjamin, Jürgen Habermas suggests that Benjamin's theses on the concept of history are essentially conservative (or conservative-revolutionary), since they imply a concept of critique which lies in the redemption of the past. Following Adorno, one might say that Benjamin's argument runs the serious risk of falling into an undialectical archaism and thus a political conservatism. And since, as Axel Honneth puts it in developing these suggestions, it is unclear to what extent it is meaningful to speak of a communicative relationship to people or groups of people who belong to the realm of the dead, beyond a methodological quasi-magical notion of 'experience', the risk of falling into a concept of the past and the dead which has little to distinguish it from a conservative politics seems to be quite high indeed.[161] In the context of the overall argument about the dead in this and the previous chapter, Habermas and Honneth's points are crucial, and raise a more general concern. For since: (i) we have moved in this chapter from positing historical materialism as a historical forgetting ('let the dead bury their dead') to suggesting that maybe historical materialism might actually constitute a form of remembering; and (ii) we moved in the last chapter to identifying a particular concept of historical tradition as the core of conservatism; and (iii) these issues in both chapters centred on a debate about our relation to the dead, then the obvious question arises: are there any grounds left which enable us to distinguish between historical materialism and conservatism on the question of remembrance? In other words, are we in danger of allowing Benjamin's arguments to take Marxism down an inherently conservative road, and thus out of Marxism altogether? For if, as Benjamin suggests, our task is to redeem some part of the past, and if, as Benjamin also suggests, we miss the opportunity to engage in such redemption then the memory of our ancestors will be irretrievably lost, then what is there to distinguish this from, say, Burke's claims about the dead within his conservative vision of tradition? Moreover, and even more dangerously, is this idea of redemption just a little too close to the fascist idea of resurrection? After all, haven't rather a lot of people described fascism itself as a form of redemptive politics?

Although one might certainly describe as 'conservative' the sort of critique which either attempts to preserve everything as a matter of principle or locates itself within the dominant tradition, none of these characteristics apply to Benjamin's idea of redemption.[162] Far from seeking to preserve everything, Benjamin wishes to preserve the struggles of the oppressed for the purpose of the contemporary revolutionary (and thus anti-tradition) movement. And far from being located in the dominant tradition, Benjamin points to the ways in which the dominant tradition is suspect precisely because of its use by 'the victors' and 'the enemy'. Far from being an end in itself, then, Benjamin seeks to use the tradition of struggles against oppression in order to avenge that very oppression, and he does this because his concept of redemption is forged through the concept of an antagonistic class society rather than an organic unity under the authority of the state.

Moreover, Benjamin constantly reiterates that the kinds of images he is talking about as the core of a materialist concept of history are simultaneously *wish images*. Anamnestic solidarity figures in Benjamin as redemptive solidarity, centred on the now-time and to be realized in the future. This image of the future is as far from conservative as can be, for it is one in which 'the collective seeks both to overcome and to transfigure the immaturity of the social product and the inadequacies in the social organization of production'. At the same time,

> what emerges in these wish images is the resolute effort to distance oneself from all that is antiquated . . . In the dream in which each epoch entertains images of its successor, the latter appears wedded to elements of primal history – that is, to elements of a classless society. And the experiences of such a society – as stored in the unconscious of the collective – engender, through interpenetration with what is new, the utopia that has left its trace in a thousand configurations of life.[163]

This is a historical futurity reminiscent of Marx's notion that the world has long possessed the dream of something which it has to become conscious of in order to actually live it. As Benjamin puts it, 'the realization of dream elements, in the course of waking up, is the paradigm of dialectical thinking'.[164] Benjamin's concept of remembrance is thus not backward-looking in any conservative sense, but futural. It is an attempt precisely to *avoid* a politics in which 'people pass things down to posterity, by making them untouchable and thus liquidating them'.[165] The angel of history may have his face turned towards the past, but the storm from Paradise irresistibly propels him into the future.

This historical futurity envisions the past as gathered up within the present in an *apocalyptic* fashion. In contrast to the historicist and conservative 'eternal' or 'immortal' image of the past, the historical materialist aims to 'blast open the continuum of history' – to 'make the continuum of history explode' rather than peddle a myth of continuity: to 'blast a specific era out of the homogeneous course of history'.[166] And the purpose of such blasts and explosions is clearly distinct from any conservative politics, for while the model of 'completion' contained within Benjamin's concept of redemption may superficially appear conservative, its ultimate aim is not for redemption as a *realizable* practical goal, but as an impulse to revolutionary action.[167] Revolutionary action, that is, towards the most communist – and thus decidedly non-conservative – idea imaginable: a classless society.

In this sense we need to read Benjamin's concept of redemption less through the lens of theology – and the inherent danger of conservatism within theology – and more through its secular connotations. Too many interpretations of Benjamin have assumed that because his argument hinges on the messianic, the concept of redemption is necessarily theological. But the theological meaning of redemption is only one of a complex set of meanings. Redemption also refers to 'the action of freeing a prisoner, captive or slave by payment', 'the action of freeing, delivering, or restoring in some way', and 'the fact of obtaining a privileged status, or admission to a society'. In political terms, then, such an act can take on the sense of 'to make good on the debts of the past', or even 'to rescue the past by means of the future'.[168] Redemption and conservatism are thus understood in political opposition: the task to be accomplished is not the conservation of the past, but rather the redemption of the hopes of the past.[169]

Far from entailing a conservative concept of historical unity or an eternal contract between generations, this argument is pitched *against* the conservative idea of reconciliation. Marx himself warned of the way in which 'lachrymose words of reconciliation' could function as an anti-revolutionary tool; the way, that is, that the search for a 'sentimental reconciliation' of contradictory class interests functions as an ideological gloss of the highest order.[170] And of the many things Benjamin expressed concern about, 'sentimental reconciliation' is fairly near the top: 'Mistrust in the fate of European literature, mistrust in the fate of freedom, mistrust in the fate of European humanity, but three times mistrust in all reconciliation: between classes, between nations, between individuals.'[171] And, of course, reconciliation between generations. For there is a fundamental – an irreconcilable – difference between reconciliation and redemption. Where reconciliation imposes a certain closure, insisting on some sort of conclusion, redemption insists on a certain openness, in the sense that the future is not wholly determined.[172] Politically, reconciliation and redemption are not compatible; they are as incompatible as conservatism and Marxism.

But there is even more at stake than simply distinguishing redemption from reconciliation and thereby laying out the ground for a historical materialist concept of the dead adequate to a revolutionary movement of the future (as though that alone is not a high enough stake). One of the reasons for Benjamin's concern with developing an account of redemption was his sense of the very real political danger of failing to do so. This danger was far greater than simply being read as presenting a 'merely' conservative position. Benjamin knew that if Marxism failed to develop a materialist politics of remembrance, then another movement would be willing to do so. In the 1920s and 1930s this enemy was winning victory after victory. It was called 'fascism'.

3 • Fascism: Long Live Death!

Benjamin's suggestion that if the fascist enemy is victorious then not even the dead will be safe plays heavily on perhaps the most common image of fascism: that it is terrifying. The image is encouraged in all sorts of ways. Key figures such as Hitler are almost always presented in the literature on fascism as a combination of homicidal maniac, despotic tyrant, racist fanatic and vicious madman. At the same time, fascism itself glorifies struggle and violence, stresses the Machiavellian point that sometimes one has to rule through fear and produces leaders who seem to love bragging about their own toughness and struggles for success. Add to this the memory of the murder of millions and fascism easily comes to figure in the political imagination as a powerful and terrifying force.

But what happens if we turn this picture on its head and think of fascism and its main protagonists not as terrifying, but as terrified? In other words, what if Hitler and other fascists are, first and foremost, simply scared?

If one reads *Mein Kampf* with this in mind one notices something rather odd: Hitler really is quite scared. In the opening chapters in particular Hitler is simply terrified. Germany and everything German is under attack. Sitting eating his lunch alone while his fellow workers eat together on the building site in Vienna, Hitler notes how the men rejected everything – the nation, fatherland, authority of the law, school, religion: 'there was absolutely nothing which was not drawn through the mud of a terrifying depth'. Social democracy is understood as an 'infamous spiritual terror', imposing 'terror at the place of employment, in the factory, in the meeting hall, and on the occasion of mass demonstrations'; trade unions are 'instruments of terror against the security and independence of the national economy'.[1] This becomes a theme of the book: the 'terrifying number' of the 'forces of decay', the 'terrible' alliance policy, the terrible half-measures against Marxism and so on.[2] And where he is not terrified, Hitler is horrified: 'I do not know what horrified me most at that time: the economic misery of my companions, their moral and ethical coarseness, or the low level of their intellectual development.' In fact, there was for Hitler horror at every turn: 'horror at such an attitude [lack of national pride]', the 'horror' of the war, the 'horror' of the quality of artistic work.[3] Hitler himself traces this back to his childhood: 'at the age of six the pitiable little boy suspects the existence of things which can inspire even an adult with nothing but horror'.[4] Regardless of whether one buys into a 'primal experience' interpretation of Hitler's horror, it is quite clear that fear is central to his whole politics and, as we shall see, the ideology of fascism.

'The statement that fear was Hitler's basic emotion may come as a surprise', says Ernst Nolte.[5] It may, but then, as I hope to show, digging into the ideology and psyche of the fascist mind reveals that this basic emotion should have been evident to us from the start. But what was there to be scared of? Nolte suggests that 'the *subject* of Hitler's fear can be easily determined, and yet it is not easy to define. It is Germany, the nation, the Fatherland.' On the other hand, 'the *object* of Hitler's fear, and hence of his hate, emerges far more often and far more clearly than its subject . . . The universal culprit was known to be the Jew.'[6] In fact, the *object* of Hitler's fear is nowhere near as clear as Nolte suggests. To be sure, the Jew is there at the heart of the fear, but Hitler's concept of the Jew was inextricably bound up – one might even say confused – with his concept of communism, democracy and finance or 'unproductive' capital. These targets are so linked in the mind of the Nazi that they are more or less the same target: the attack on unproductive or finance capital forms part of the attack on Jewish capital, and yet the attack on the Jew is simultaneously an attack on communism. For Nazism, there existed a Jewish–Bolshevik world conspiracy which was using democracy as a mechanism for the domination of finance capitalism, an ideological conglomerate which required new discursive formations such as 'Jewish FinanceBolshevism' or 'Marxian-demoralizing-Liberal-Capitalistic' to capture the combination of Jew, capitalist, liberal-democratic and communist enemy.

The object of Hitler's fear might be the Jew, then, but it is never *clearly* the Jew, for this object possesses contradictory qualities: a communist intent on overthrowing private property and yet also a capitalist consumed by greed; a figure with too much public influence and yet who retreats into his private sphere; a force behind the institutions of the modern state and yet which also threatens to abolish them once in full control; an avant-garde artist with extravagant and subversive values and yet also a provincial petty-bourgeois white-collar worker; pacifist and yet belligerent imperialist; homosexual ruining

strong masculinity and yet seducer of Aryan women. The list of
contradictions goes on and on. Worse, this figure appears to slip from
being a race, a religion, a culture or a nation (or even variety of nations),
and back again. The enemy, in other words, is engaged in an *endless
mimesis*. The power of this enemy lies in its mimetic being, and thus
the ability to insert itself into every culture, state and social grouping,
and to live a life parasitic upon these, constantly threatening them
with bastardization.[7] The enemy begins to look like the most complex
hybrid form ever seen and, partly because of its complexity and partly
because of the assumption that it has hidden powers and agents secreted
everywhere, the fear is constantly being interpreted and reinterpreted,
a process which itself confirms and intensifies the fear.[8] Thus the
object of Hitler's fear is not at all clear because the object appears to
have no clear identity. The enemy is a formless entity transgressing all
borders and resisting all forms of classification, constantly changing in
order to disguise itself and to hide the nature of its attack. Worse still,
the enemy object has 'taken on a human look'.[9] As fascists from Hitler
to Carl Schmitt never tire of pointing out, not every being with a human
face is human.[10] But the human appearance helps disguise the fact that
the enemy is in fact – again contradictorily – both superhuman and
subhuman: it possesses superhuman powers enabling it to drive the
world to perdition and yet is also a subhuman cause of degeneration,
disease and disintegration: 'the anti-man, the creature of another god
. . . a creature outside nature and alien to nature'.[11] Images of superhuman
power and subhuman pestilence are contrary representations, but fascism
attributed both to one and the same being, as though an endlessly
changing and endlessly mimetic force had launched a constantly shifting
offensive against humanity.[12] As Saul Friedländer puts it:

> Many of the images, not only in Hitler's vision of the Jew but also in anti-
> Semitism generally, seem to converge in such constant transformations.
> These images are the undistorted echo of past representations of the Jew as
> endlessly changing and endlessly the same, a living dead, either a ghostly
> wanderer or a ghostly ghetto inhabitant. Thus the all-pervasive Jewish
> threat becomes in fact formless and unrepresentable; as such it leads to the
> most frightening phantasm of all: a threat that looms everywhere, that,
> although it penetrates everything, is an invisible carrier of death.[13]

This endless mimesis and ability to be everywhere and nowhere, to be
everything and nothing, superhuman and subhuman, is what Stephen

Eric Bronner has called the chameleon-effect: the enemy was thought to have such an overwhelming power because it is a chameleon capable of taking different forms at different times.[14] We might say that a better suggestion is that the enemy is a monster.

Despite the specifically named targets discussed in *Mein Kampf* – Jews, communists, parliamentarians and so on – the enemy is most commonly thought of as some kind of monster. Hitler comments on his early development into politics that when he first began reading accounts of the Jewish question 'the whole thing seemed to me so monstrous . . . that, tormented by the fear of doing injustice, I again became anxious and uncertain'.[15] Although this initial anxiety and uncertainty did not turn him away from politics, he was soon to encounter monster after monster in his battle to save the German nation. From *Mein Kampf* to *Table Talk* via the 'Secret Book' of 1928 and a whole host of speeches, the enemy is always an 'amorphous monster'.[16] The Jewish faith is 'positively monstrous'.[17] Princes who suck the blood from their people are 'monsters . . . who torment the "beloved people" to despair'.[18] Marxism, the 'Red Monster', could have been produced 'only in the brains of a monster – not that of a man',[19] a product no doubt of an education system which 'succeeds only in producing intellectual monsters'.[20] The declaration of a German Republic in 1918 is seen as 'a monstrous event' following monstrous bloodshed, and the resulting monstrous war reparations gave birth to a 'monster-child'. Democracy and parliamentarianism are likewise said to have created 'a "monstrosity of excrement and fire" '.[21]

We could go on in this vein. Russia and the Jews have created 'a super-industrialised monster'.[22] What about the United States? 'Monster is the only possible name for it.'[23] The state as it is generally conceived is for Hitler 'the greatest monstrosity of the twentieth century'.[24] For Nazism the state is a means to an end – the preservation and advancement of racial groups. In this sense the state is for Hitler a 'living organism of a nationality', an *organic* force in the struggle between races.[25] And 'states which do not serve this purpose are misbegotten, monstrosities in fact'.[26] They are monstrosities because they are viewed and used in purely *mechanistic* terms. The order of the day is 'preservation at any price of the current monstrosity of human mechanism, now called state'.[27] Nietzsche was thus right in describing the state as 'the coldest of all cold monsters': what 'they [the Marxist-liberal-democratic-Jewish theorists] try to palm off on us as a state today is usually nothing but a monstrosity born of deepest human

error'.[28] Unsurprisingly, most of the policies which emerge from such a
state are nothing other than 'programmatical *monstrosities*'.[29]

This idea of an amorphous monstrous enemy permeated far-right
discourse in the first half of the twentieth century, continues to
permeate such discourse today and both then and now has fed into the
fascist imagination. It can be found, for example, in the 'male fantasies'
of the Freikorps documented by Klaus Theweleit. The combination
(again: ever-shifting, mimetic, chameleon-like) of the proletarian,
communist, sexually active woman undermining German order and
decency conjures up images of a certain kind of woman: simultaneously
sexually and politically active and thus politically and sexually threatening. In the male fantasies explored by Theweleit such women are
described as having disgusting features: screeching and laughing, red
in face if not body, naked and pleased with it, devoid of all feelings
and respect; to the men in question they are truly monstrous.
Theweleit argues that

> the description of the proletarian woman as monster . . . can be traced to an
> attempt to construct a fantastic being who swears, shrieks, spits, scratches,
> farts, bites, pounces, tears to shreds; who is slovenly, wind-whipped,
> hissing-red, indecent; who whores around, slaps its naked thighs, and can't
> get enough of laughing at these men.[30]

> Revulsion at these monsters-of-the-imagination, 'proletarian women' and
> 'female communists', is no doubt related to sexual ideas that are charged
> with even more intense anxieties, so great that they cannot be expressed.
> 'Proletarian woman' seems to be the name for a horror that is in fact
> unnameable . . . Just what that horror might be, remains unclear.[31]

Again, the lack of clarity means that this monstrous form could slide
easily into all the others in far-right discourse of the period.

Do the phantasmatic representations ever have a name? Occasionally
Hitler's 'monster' appears as the hydra: as communist and capitalist,
homosexual and rabid heterosexual, and so on, 'the Jewish world
hydra' appears a monster with many heads and with the capability of
replacing those heads torn off in battle.[32] But I want to explore the
possibility that the real monster for fascism is none other than the
vampire. We know from the previous chapter that there is plenty of
political mileage in vampires, but that for Marx the image was in no
way associated with Jews. The argument in this chapter will therefore

allow some important comparisons with Marx's use of the vampire and illustrate the ways in which certain monstrous forms can be used for very different political ends. At the same time, it will again lead into a discussion of the dead, where the argument will present a very different politics of the dead to that we have encountered thus far.

The thrill of horror

To understand the development of the idea of the vampiric and monstrous Jew we need to step back a little into the development of anti-Semitism in the nineteenth century. I have argued elsewhere that the emergence of fascism and modern anti-Semitism has to be understood in the context of the development of nationalism and 'race-thinking' in the late nineteenth century, and in particular the way that questions of class interacted with questions of nation and race.[33] But this context also needs to be connected to the changing nature of the Gothic in this same period.

The development and consolidation of the nation-state in the nineteenth century led to the Jewish people being thought of as a people without a nation. Worse, Jewish settlement in diverse areas meant the Jews could be thought of as a nation within other nations – an essentially 'homeless' nation – and thus a 'parasite' in the body of other nations and states. The Jew came to be thought of as a foreigner like no other foreigner, for not only was the Jew not at home in Germany, but the Jew was not at home anywhere. Being a foreigner was thought to be the *essence* of the Jew rather than a transitory state. As such, the Jew could easily be thought of as posing a double threat. On the one hand, the Jew stubbornly refuses to adopt *the* mode of being, to adhere to *the* political form through which rootedness should be expressed. Instead they insist on being a 'community' within other nations. On the other hand, being a non-national nation meant that the Jews were equally an inter-national nation, in that their nation-less state allowed them to drift across the borders of other, real nations. Since the nation was to be the basis of salvation, the medium through which rejuvenation and revitalization could occur, the Jew's lack of nation threatens this salvation from within, so to speak. Moreover, the Jews' preaching of universal human values was also thought to undermine the nation, for the Jew appears intellectually committed to a universalism which pits free will and the idea of choice – either through a commitment to universal liberal values of Enlightenment reason or to Marxist internationalism – against the mythic status of national boundaries. Both physically and intellectually the Jew defies the truth on which all nations rest their claims: the naturally ascribed character of nationhood and the naturalness of the national form.

This tension around the status of the Jew vis-à-vis the nation-state intensified during the heyday of imperialism from the mid-1880s through to the outbreak of the First World War. Integral to this intensification was the way in which race-thinking both connected with and subsumed some of the parallel tensions around classes, nations and their struggles. During the late nineteenth century race-thinking became more explicitly political in that the idea of race and racial superiority came to figure as an ideological mechanism that enabled individuals – and often and perhaps especially oppressed individuals – to feel part of a racial aristocracy. In the case of the working class, for example, the idea that there are fundamental differences between races which allows us to arrange them hierarchically presents an image of and to the white working class that it too is part of a higher race. By positing racial struggle as the driving force of history, the working class can be conceptualized as part of a new racial aristocracy and thus, in terms of the nineteenth century, part of the driving force of history. The message to the worker then, is: why identify with an oppressed class when you can identify with the (racial) aristocracy? Racism thereby becomes a powerful ideological substitute for the class struggle, the racial other being the new enemy for the newly unified peoples' community and, at the same time, an equally powerful underlying factor in the imperialist drive. Through this set of tensions concerning race and class ran the theme of blood. Foucault has argued that, in the second half of the nineteenth century, the theme of blood was called on to lend ideological weight toward revitalizing the type of political power that was exercised through the devices of sexuality. Racism took shape at this point, out of which a series of permanent interventions at the level of the body, conduct, health and everyday life received their justification from the mythical concern with the purity of the blood and the triumph of the race.[34] But we need to add to Foucault's account the fact that because class was increasingly seen through the racial lens, so class also came to be seen through the prism of blood. As Benedict Anderson notes, 'the dreams of racism actually have their origin in ideologies of *class* . . . above all in claims to divinity among rulers and to "blue" or "white" blood and "breeding" among aristocracies'.[35]

Now, it was during this period that a shift also took place in the Gothic tradition. Cultural historians of the Gothic have shown how the terrain of Gothic horror shifted from the fear of corrupted aristocracy or clergy, represented by the haunted castle or abbey, to the fear embodied by monstrous bodies within the domestic sphere – where 'domestic' has a useful ambiguity pointing to the 'private' sphere on the one hand (family, home) and the national as opposed to 'foreign' on the other. As part of this shift the question of *aristocratic* heritage became less and less of an index of national identity, being gradually usurped by a newer form of national identity increasingly dependent upon the category of race. The blood of nobility came to be thought through in terms of the blood of the national citizen, and both came to be identified in terms of their distinctness from so-called 'impure' races such as Jews and gypsies. As imperialism progressed abroad and national identity developed as a means for subduing class struggle at 'home', non-nationals came to be identified by their alien natures and monstrous features. This broad social, economic and political environment of the late nineteenth century laid the foundation for the ascendancy of the vampire theme. For as the concept 'foreign' became increasingly associated with a kind of parasitical monstrosity, so Gothic monsters in this period made parasitism – and thus vampirism – the defining characteristic of horror.[36] Thus the cultural understanding of monstrosity was contemporaneous with, intersected with and participated in socio-political theories of racial superiority. Let me flesh this idea out through a brief discussion of this period's best-known and most popular work in the Gothic genre – Bram Stoker's *Dracula* (1897).

As is well-known, *Dracula* is a story of purity and danger. But it is a story of purity and danger which needs to be put in the context of both the large number of foreign Jews in England in the later part of the nineteenth century and Stoker's personal affiliations – Stoker was good friends with Richard Burton, author of a tract reviving the blood libel against Jews. Dracula is in many ways a caricatured personification of Jewish character: his physical characteristics, his relation to money, his parasitism and his moral degeneracy all mark him out as in some way Jewish.

Jonathan Harker's description of Dracula in the opening section of the novel bears testimony to the Count's 'very marked physiognomy', including an aquiline face with a long thin nose with arched nostrils, massive eyebrows and thick, curly hair, a cruel mouth and peculiarly sharp white teeth, pointed ears and an 'extraordinary pallor'.[37] While several of his physical features might be interpreted as signs of Jewishness, his features change throughout the novel – a sign of the vampire's mimetic faculty (to the extent that he can even appear in London as an Englishman) – but on all occasions the suggestion is of a certain Jewishness. Comments from other characters reinforce the association of Dracula with Jewish physiognomy. One of the workers who drags the coffins to Dracula's castle comments that 'the place was so neglected that yer might 'ave smelled ole Jerusalem in it'. It is also an unscrupulous Jew who helps Dracula escape his hunters: 'we found Hildescheim in his office, a Hebrew of rather the Adelphi Theatre type, with a nose like a sheep, and a fez . . . With a little bargaining he told us what he knew' (448). Either way, Dracula is definitely East European and thus very foreign. It is clear from the opening page that we are in an 'orientalist' text. Entering the world of Dracula means 'leaving the West and entering the East' (7), and this strangeness or 'otherness' is commented on throughout the novel in terms of, for example, the food Dracula eats, his table manners, the way he sleeps, his strange smell, his aversion to the cross and his burial customs. Dracula is thus not only Jewish, but is also essentially foreign – he is simply 'the other' (374). It is Dracula's status as a foreign invader that helps establish his monstrosity in the novel. It also sets him apart from many other Gothic creations and makes him truly uncanny (*unheimlich*) – Dracula not only leaves his own home but also appears to wish to make everywhere his 'home', a kind of 'supernatural imperialism'.[38]

This supernatural imperialism is reinforced by Dracula's tendency to hoard gold and foreign currency. On searching Dracula's castle Harker discovers 'a great heap of gold in one corner' and money from several nations: 'gold of all kinds, Roman, and British, and Austrian, and Hungarian, and Greek and Turkish money' (66). It is the threat to this money when confronted by his pursuers that makes the usually cool Dracula finally lose control – 'the expression of the Count's face was so hellish, that for a moment I feared for Harker' – and willing to risk his 'life' to save it: 'The next instant, with a sinuous dive he swept under Harker's arm, ere his blow could fall, and, grasping a handful of the money from the floor, dashed across the room, threw himself at the window.' And this is a creature who not only craves money, but appears to be made of it: 'The point [of the blade] just cut the cloth of his coat, making a wide gap whence a bundle of bank-notes and a stream of gold fell out' (394). The allusion here is thus to a being so closely identified with money that it runs through their veins.

This allusion is no doubt connected to the battle over blood which permeates the novel. Culturally and politically blood is often connected to different things: food and nourishment, semen, the blood of Christ, life and death (and, of course, capital). But its meaning also depends on the ways in which it has become a crucial identifier and metaphor for racial identity. The fact that much of the novel turns on the question of blood is central to this combined development, especially given the intensification of the political importance of blood to the nationalist and far-right agenda during the late nineteenth century. Dracula announces early on that 'the warlike days are over. Blood is too precious a thing in these days of dishonourable peace' (43). In contrast, his own people 'have a right to be proud, for in our veins flows the blood of many brave races who fought as the lion fights, for lordship' (42). Likewise, when the degenerate Renfield goes mad he simply keeps repeating 'The blood is the life! The blood is the life!' (184). And when he is sufficiently *compos mentis* to explain himself he does so in the terms central to the novel: 'On one occasion I tried to kill him [Jonathan Harker] for the purpose of strengthening my vital powers by the assimilation with my own body of his life through the medium of his blood – relying, of course, upon the Scriptural phrase, "For the blood is the life" ' (301).

The biblical idiom masks the political dimension to the comment, a dimension easily identified in the way the question of blood functions as a mechanism for incorporating the question of gender and sexuality into the novel. The two women on whom the Count focuses in the novel, Lucy Westenra (the occidental name reinforcing the orientalist theme) and Mina Harker, both represent modern women. Lucy describes herself as a 'horrid flirt' in love with three men, and even wonders 'why can't they let a girl marry three men, or as many as want her . . .? But this is heresy, and I must not say it' (81). Mina ponders on the question of the 'New Woman' and the question of whether some day men and women might be 'allowed to see each other asleep before proposing or accepting', and that the New Woman might actually propose to the man herself (119). Thus on the one hand there are two very 'modern' women, and it is relevant that during the early twentieth century the term 'vampire' increasingly came to refer once again to sexually predatory women – the 'vamp' – who had emanated from the socialist masses to wreak a sexual-political havoc upon the order of male power. This lent ideological weight to those who fought against female sexual emancipation, for as Bram Dijkstra argues, the political obsession with blood was 'instrumental in turning any woman who exhibited even the slightest independent interest in sex into a vampire'.[39] On the other hand there is Dracula's desire for 'our' women. When Dracula makes off with the money he speaks not of his desire for wealth but for foreign women: 'Your girls that you all love are mine already; and through them you and others shall yet be mine' (394). And much of the novel is spent exploring the ways in which Dracula needs to seek out English women, drink their blood and make them his. The 'mine' here captures the combination of possession and the fact that when Dracula consumes the blood of a person his victim not only becomes a vampire but also takes on a new racial identity. Moreover, the process of sexual possession is decidedly not 'normal', since Dracula's sexual predatoriness is expressed through a combination of oral fixation and necrophilia. The strangeness which makes Dracula so monstrous is thus doubly frightening: not only does he seek the money and property which gives him power, he is also the foreigner whose invasion is also intended to be specifically and perversely sexual. His supernatural imperialism is simultaneously a sexual imperialism.

This struggle over the sexuality of women is also resolved through the battle of blood. When Lucy succumbs to the Count she is given blood from her three suitors and then yet another male. No woman can be trusted to provide the blood, for it has to be a male and heterosexual union/transfusion: 'a brave man's blood is the best thing on this earth when a woman is in trouble . . . You are a man, and it is a man we want' (159, 194). Fed by the blood of four men, Lucy becomes the kind of woman she wished to be – to have as many men as want her. But this merely turns her into a wild woman, so wild in fact that her desires can only be satisfied by the blood of children, and she degenerates into a primal bestiality. To stop Lucy sating her lust on children, the four men who have provided the blood-semen come together to execute her, a process through which Lucy regains her true femininity. 'There in the coffin lay no longer the foul Thing that we had so dreaded and grown to hate . . . but Lucy as we had seen her in her life, with her face of unequaled sweetness and purity.' Thus Lucy is transformed from degenerate wild woman of unbridled desire to that ideal creature of feminine virtue: the dead woman.

Unsurprisingly, Stoker has been accused of writing a book which was to become 'the basic commonplace book of the anti-feminine obsession' – a 'cautionary tale directed to men of the modern temper, warning them not to yield to the bloodlust of the feminist, the new Woman'.[40] The broader point, however, is to link this anti-feminine obsession to the more general issues concerning racial and national identity that are played out in the novel. In making this link it becomes clear that *Dracula* occupies a crucial turning point in the vampire literature. Whereas previously it had been the case that vampires had been associated with a particular class – either aristocratic or bourgeois (or even subversive underclass) depending on one's reading, as we saw in the previous chapter – *Dracula* transforms the threat from a particular class into a threat to money, women, order and stability posed by the degenerate foreigner.[41] In presenting chaos or disorder as the product of a monstrous invasion of England, *Dracula* subsumes the socio-political threat posed by a class under the threat posed to the nation by 'alien' powers. As such, the question of one class 'living' off the blood of another class is transformed into a question of the unclean otherness in the bad blood of race. *Dracula* performs here an important function in relation to the development of 'race-thinking' in the nineteenth century. Just as key texts on races and racial inequality such as Count Arthur de Gobineau's *Essay on the Inequality of the Human Races* (1853) had sought the solution to the 'fall of civilization' and the 'decadence' associated with such a fall in the creation of a new elite *race*, so the same ideology came to be found in popular Gothic literature such as *Dracula*. Thus the novel offers a list of once 'proud' and 'brave' races which have since fallen from power and even from history: Berserkers, Magyars, Romans, Danes and Vikings. As Stephen Arata puts it, Dracula

> is dangerous as the representative or embodiment of a race which, all evidence suggested, was poised to 'step forward' and become 'masters' of those who had already 'spent their strength'. Even Dracula's destruction (which, if he stands in for an entire race, becomes a fantasized genocide) cannot entirely erase the moral endorsed by the rest of the story: that strong races inevitably weaken and fall, and are in turn displaced by stronger races.[42]

This question of race accounts for the question of degeneracy in the novel, which correlates with an emergent nationalist and eventually fascist concern with the issue from this period onwards. The various ambiguities of representation in the novel are bound up with the

ambiguities in the wider discourse of degeneration throughout the
period in which the novel was written and became popular. Stoker was
a believer in physiognomy and avid reader of the work on degeneracy
then common; he had apparently read Max Nordau's *Degeneration*
(1893, translated 1895) with bated breath.[43] Unsurprisingly, the vampire's
'otherness' is integrally linked to the question of degeneracy. Dracula
is genetically 'predestinate to crime' and has a 'child-brain'. As the
character Van Helsing puts it, 'The Count is a criminal and of criminal
type. Nordau and Lombroso would so classify him, and *qua* criminal
he is of imperfectly formed mind' (439). Likewise, the subplot in-
volving the degenerate madman Renfield is clearly meant to show that
such degenerate characters can be used by the vampire for their work
(Renfield: 'I am here to do your bidding Master' (135)). As Daniel Pick
points out, 'the image of the parasite and the blood-sucker informed
late nineteenth-century eugenics and the biological theory of degeneration', which in turn then fed into novels about blood-suckers.[44]
The key texts which were to provide the ideological foundations of
fascism, from Gobineau's *Inequality of the Human Races* to Nordau's
Degeneration and Houston Stewart Chamberlain's *Foundations of the
Nineteenth Century* (1899), together helped shape the fear of the
monstrous products of degeneration, a process in which Stoker's novel
played its part.

On the one hand, then, *Dracula* occupies a crucial cultural space
and fundamental turning point in the Gothic novel. Its portrayal of
foreignness, Jews, gypsies, degeneration, money and sexually predatory
'New' women in the form of the vampire, sustained through pseudo-
scientific theories of degeneracy and criminality, represented a major
shift in the subject and object of the vampire novel. But on the other
hand, and also more important to the argument here, we might also
say that it presents an important *Gothic opening* for racism and anti-
Semitism. From here on in, 'degenerate' races in general, Jews in
particular and any other 'threats' to the nation could and would be
thought of via Gothic tropes and techniques – as nothing less than
political monstrosities. In an interview in 1977 Michel Foucault was
quizzed about his interest in blood in *The History of Sexuality*.
Foucault comments that, while historians of the nobility were singing
the praises of noble blood, what was new in the nineteenth century
was the appearance of a racist biology centered around the related
concepts of degeneracy and blood. There then takes place the following
exchange:

Guy Le Gaufey [one of the interviewers]: Couldn't one see a confirmation
of what you are saying in the nineteenth century vogue for vampire novels,
in which the aristocracy is always presented as the beast to be destroyed?
The vampire is always an aristocrat, and the saviour a bourgeois.
Foucault: In the eighteenth century, rumours were already circulating that
debauched aristocrats abducted little children to slaughter them and
regenerate themselves by bathing in their blood.
Le Gaufey: Yes, but that's only the beginning. The way the idea becomes
extended is strictly bourgeois, with that whole literature of vampires whose
themes recur in films today: it's always the bourgeois, without the resources
of the police or the curé, who gets rid of the vampire.
Foucault: Modern antisemitism began in that form.45

Foucault and Le Gaufey here pick up on the way the vampire novel
forms part of the overlap between the development of modern anti-
Semitism and the Gothic form. The novel facilitated the ideological
displacement of perceived social and political dangers on to the horror
story of a foreign agent of destruction and disorder. The novel, in other
words, helped in the development of the ideological ploy in which social
and political dangers posed by a parasitic race could be presented in
Gothic terms. Thus in the same period in which Jewish and racial
others were being increasingly represented in Gothic fiction as horrific
and monstrous, so politically the racial and Jewish other was increasingly
Gothicized – transformed into a monstrous figure horrifying the
community. By creating the idea of the Jew as a supernatural creature,
Gothic anti-Semitism helped develop the idea of Jews and their
associated forces and alliances as monstrous.

As far as I know, there is no evidence that Hitler was familiar with
Dracula. But let us briefly play around with some possibilities. In
Dracula, Stoker has Van Helsing comment that vampires do not die,
but go on adding new victims and multiplying their forces: 'They
become *nosferatu*, as they call it in Eastern Europe' (275–6). In 1922
Nosferatu hit the screens in Germany. Made by F. W. Murnau in a
departure from his usual work producing propaganda films for the
German war effort, it was based (heavily or very loosely according to
one's interpretation) on *Dracula*. Made twenty-five years after the
publication of the book, it follows for the most part the form and
structure of the novel, but with some differences. A recently married
clerk of an estate agent is sent to Count Graf Orlok's castle to settle a
property deal. At night, Orlok, a bald, hunched figure with pointed
ears, rat teeth, hook-nose and ever-growing fingernails on hands that

he dangles in front of him like paws, approaches the clerk to suck his blood. The clerk's wife Ellen awakens in Bremen and calls her husband's name. At this moment Orlok withdraws from the victim – the power of real love between man and woman has saved the victim from the vampire. The clerk returns to Bremen, while Orlok leaves the castle to haunt the world. His association with the plague means that wherever he goes, people die – when his coffins are opened by the crew of a ship plague-carrying rats emerges from the dirt within. Indeed, far more deaths result from the fact that he carries the plague than from the fact that he drinks blood. (Stoker's suggestion that 'nosferatu' was how the undead were known in Eastern Europe is misleading – 'nosferatu' was in fact a term derived from an Old Slavonic word, *nosufuratu*, associated with carriers of the plague.[46]) He finally encounters Ellen in Bremen who, instead of fleeing, welcomes him into her room. Ellen has discovered that the only way for the vampire and thus the plague to be destroyed is for a woman 'of pure heart' to give herself to the vampire all night so that he will forget to leave before the sun rises. She therefore decides to sacrifice herself as a civic duty, giving rise to a climactic scene in which self-sacrificial German femininity is simultaneously seduced by and yet overcomes the Jewish vampire until he can be exterminated by the sunlight of manhood. She thus falls victim and yet destroys the vampire. Only then does the sun break through in the film.

Nosferatu is interesting in both its continuities and discontinuities with *Dracula*. The only text that *Nosferatu* takes from *Dracula* is the pronouncement that 'the blood is the life!' The film not only portrays a 'typical' German town under foreign threat, it also stresses the foreign nature of the vampire. The character Renfield is no longer a madman but is now a real estate agent, seen engaging with the Count in a private transaction over sheets of paper with foreign writing. Like the Count, Renfield is also bald, hunched and seemingly obsessed. The plague thus comes to the German town through the collusion of Renfield with the Count. That is, the plague is brought to the innocent German town from a foreign nation by a monstrous figure engaged in property-dealing, putting the German inhabitants at the mercy of the property-acquiring Jew-like figure of the vampire. As Ken Gelder points out, 'given the appearance of Nosferatu [Orlok] and the connection to Renfield – who helps him purchase German property – it is, in fact, difficult *not* to see this German film as anti-Semitic'.[47] Bram Dijkstra suggests that, whereas in *Dracula* the erotic depredations of the Semitic vampire still took precedence, in *Nosferatu* it is the *economic* eroticism of the vampire which takes centre stage.[48] But it is surely more the case that, as for fascism generally, the sexual vampire and racial vampire both overlap with the economic vampire, all of which are encoded within a broader conception of the vampire's *foreignness*: a pestilence which comes in the form of a sexually predatory blood-sucking and property-developing tyrant looming at the borders of the nation.

We do not know if Hitler saw *Nosferatu*, but the film remains a fundamental expression of the kinds of fears which preoccupied nationalist, racist and anti-Semitic tendencies during the period, playing a role similar to that of *Dracula*. The conflation of ideas concerning race, property and gender that came to form the basis of the National Socialist programme was central to Murnau's film, whose central figure can be read as an indicator of the political blend of cultural metaphors crucial in the triumph of Nazism, and which runs through a range of cultural productions, from Artur Dinter's novel *The Sin Against the Blood* (1918, selling 260,000 copies by 1934) to the equally popular *Vampir* (1920) by Hanns Heinz Ewers.[49] 'During this period', Siegfried Kracauer writes, 'German imagination, regardless of its starting-point, always gravitated towards such figures.'[50] Films like *Nosferatu* and novels such as those mentioned helped establish the cultural, ideological and visual context – a Gothic context – for the racial melodrama that the Nazis were about to unleash on Europe.

As with most melodramas, fear was crucial to the emotive and imaginative dimensions of the narrative. But given what was about to follow, fear had to be not just manipulated, as is commonly suggested, but politically constructed. 'The world can only be ruled by fear', Hitler tells us. The cultivation of fear thus became one of fascism's key ideological tools. 'People need wholesome fear. They *want* to fear something. They want someone to frighten them . . . The masses want that. They need something that will give them a thrill of horror.'[51] This political construction of fear, ideologically and culturally centred on an imagined monstrous assault and alien penetration of the social body, might be described as one of the foundation stones of fascist ideology. The range of fears with which this chapter began – of degeneration and democracy, of Marxism and communist trade unionism, of the lack of pride or honour – was thus transposed onto the masses as a political project. Fear was thus made to permeate the psychic life of the masses. Terror is sometimes never more powerful

than in its psychic manifestations, and what better way to access these
than through popular fantasies.[52] And since, for Nazism, blood is
indeed the life,[53] what better way to construct fears than through ideas
such as monstrous blood-suckers and vampiric parasites. Bram
Dijkstra comments that 'Hitler's focus on terms such as "bloodsucker"
and "people's vampire" to identify the Jew deliberately exploited the
same popular sources Murnau used to identify the horror of
Dracula.'[54] We might just as easily say that such terms helped
construct the fear in the first place. Either way, it is not unreasonable
to view films such as *Nosferatu* as one of the many cultural and
ideological expressions of the fascist imagination, exhibiting the kind
of nationalism and racism which became such powerful ideological
tools from the late nineteenth century onwards and which reached its
climax in Europe in the 1920s and 1930s. The fear of a monstrous and
vampiric force threatening national stability and racial purity that had
been developing in this period took its final and climatic turn when it
became the organizing principle of fascism.

'As for death – that we do fabulously!'

What might be done about such a monster? On one occasion Hitler
hits a note of optimism: 'after the death of his victim, the vampire
sooner or later dies too'.[55] But without wishing to scare Hitler too
much, one has to ask the question: does this monster ever die? There is
a sense in which, in saying that the enemy will sooner or later die,
Hitler misunderstands his own position on death. This position, I
suggest, is that the enemy *never* really dies. A sense of this idea can be
grasped in the practice of desecrating graves, which began in Europe in
the 1920s and which continues to this day. As I asked in the
Introduction, why do fascists love desecrating graves? The interpretation
given by the mainstream media and liberal intelligentsia presents grave
desecration as a senseless and offensive act of pointless violence
designed to upset civilized sensibilities and illustrating just how far
fascism is beyond the social democratic pale. Part of my intention here
will be to suggest that there is a lot more to grave desecration than this
interpretation suggests. Grave desecration, I will claim, takes us to one
of the core dimensions of fascist ideology: the dead. And it is this core
dimension of fascist ideology I want to unpick in what remains of this
book, for it reveals some of the central dynamics of fascism as an

ideology and a movement. It also will allow us to draw Marx and Burke back into the picture.

Saul Friedlander once wrote that

> to understand the phantasms that underlay many Germans' relationship to Hitler, the frenzy of their applause, their attachment to him until the last moment, it is necessary to take into account their perverse rapport with a chief and a system for reasons that certainly were not explicit and would not have shown in an opinion poll: the yearning for destruction and death.[56]

I am not convinced Friedlander does this in his book, and I have neither space nor inclination to discuss the 'yearning' of 'many Germans'. But Friedlander nonetheless hits an important nail on the head: to understand fascism, one has to think through the question of the dead. That the dead play an important role in fascism is clear from many of its texts. In *Mein Kampf* Hitler comments that one of his main aims is 'venerating those who traveled the bitter road of death for their German people'. Commenting on the post-war settlement in which four years of war brought nothing more than universal suffrage, Hitler accuses the politicians of 'vile banditry' in 'steal[ing] the war aim of the dead heroes from their very graves',[57] and warns that 'if the two million who lie buried in Flanders and Belgium were to rise from the dead' they would regard the whole post-war settlement as treason.[58] Hitler here picks up on what will become a key theme within fascist ideology: the war dead. Alfred Rosenberg's *Myth of the Twentieth Century*, for example, is dedicated to the memory of the two million Germans who fell in the First World War. Rosenberg claims that the 'stab in the back' following the First World War might well be the basis for a new movement:

> in the bowed souls of the surviving kin of the dead warriors, that mythos of the blood for which the heroes died was renewed, deepened, comprehended and experienced in its most profound ramifications . . . The mythos of the German people demands that the two million dead heroes have not fallen in vain.[59]

In one sense Hitler and Rosenberg are here saying nothing particularly original. A range of historians have shown that the dead constituted a formidable problem for both the authorities and the people – what to do with the bodies, what kind of cemeteries could be used, whether bodies could be later exhumed and reburied, and, importantly, what practices of commemoration might be acceptable. The body of the dead soldier became in all European countries an icon that carried the meaning of the war back home, an emblem in the political culture of ancestor worship that constitutes a crucial dimension of nationalist politics, and a key signifier of the new democracy of death – although it is notable that the emerging Soviet Union was content to let the dead bury their dead while getting on with the revolution.[60] The far right, however, turned the dead into a central component of the fascist movement.

In Italy after the war, for example, different towns and communes approached the question of the dead very differently depending on their local, political, anti-militarist or Catholic traditions. But any such differences were soon set aside by the fascists after 1922, who increasingly imposed their own view and practices on the diverse local initiatives.[61] This was part of a much wider strategy turning the war dead into a key fascist symbol. Only two months after seizing power the fascist regime in Italy distributed a circular suggesting the creation of Avenues of Remembrance across the country and the refashioning of existing cemeteries into Parks of Remembrance. Italy also developed and reconstructed its military cemeteries throughout the fascist regime and passed laws such as that for the 'definitive systematization of the corpses of the fallen' (June 1931). In Germany the memory of the dead was kept continuously alive through pilgrimages and ceremonials until the outbreak of the Second World War. It was thus in the name of the war dead, the unknown soldier – the 'trenchocracy' as Mussolini liked to call it[62] – that fascism sought to defend the nation and build a movement for achieving national greatness again. Moreover, stressing this was a way for a rising movement to distinguish itself simultaneously from liberal ideas about the cult of the fallen soldier and from any form of materialist – for which read 'Marxist' – politics. The point was made by fascist art critic Margherita Sarfatti in her 1925 biography of Mussolini:

> It seemed as though materialism was in the ascendant . . . when suddenly there came an awakening of the spirit. Had not men alike been in the trenches? Had not one and all been moved by the same instincts to face death for the common cause? . . . Thus musing, the nations singled out for their ideal of heroism the humble figure of the Unknown Warrior.[63]

Part of this special significance was to turn the dead into heroes. Even before the Nazi seizure of power, those on the far right were proclaiming the political and historical significance of those who died at Langemarck. Josef Magnus Wehner gave a speech of dedication at one memorial in 1932: 'The dying sang! The stormers sang. The young students sang as they were being annihilated: "Deutschland, Deutschland über alles, über alles in der Welt" . . . The dead heroes became an omen for the German people.'[64] Fascism turned such ideas into a philosophy of life, with the coming new age to be founded on the heroism of the dead. The myth of Langemarck, for example, quickly became a basic component in the repertoire of National Socialist propaganda, with annual ceremonies and eminent figures such as Martin Heidegger addressing rallies on the historic event.

In standard mythology, the hero tends to be either an exceptional being or an ordinary being who performs an exceptional act which benefits mankind; and note too that in standard mythology the hero is often one who battles the monster. For fascism, however, *everybody* is to be educated to become a hero. But if everyone is educated to become a hero, and only the dead are the truly heroic, then everyone must be being educated for death. Gregor Ziemer's research into how Nazis were being 'made' in Germany in the 1930s is telling here. Calling his book *Education for Death*, Ziemer comments that during his time in Nazi Germany he

> visited institutions of every nature: . . . schools for infants, schools for the feeble-minded, schools and institutions for boys and girls of all ages, colleges, and colonial schools. I took reams of notes, which I wrote out in detail at the earliest convenience . . . And I drew one conclusion. Hitler's schools do their jobs diabolically well. They are obeying the Fuehrer. They are educating boys and girls for death.[65]

This is clear from the popular songs produced by and for the fascist movements:

> Clear the streets, the SS marches . . .
> Let death be our battle companion
> We are the Black Band.[66]

The chorus of 'Heroic Thirds', a Spanish hymn to the Legionnaires, ran:

> Legionaries to fight
> Legionaries to die.
> Legionaries to fight
> Legionaries to die.

The Romanian Iron Guard similarly liked to sing:

> Death, only legionary death
> Is a gladsome wedding for us
> The legionary dies singing
> The legionary sings dying.[67]

Such songs were by no means restricted to the military. One pre-school nursery song ran as follows:

> We love our Führer,
> We honour our Führer,
> We follow our Führer,
>   Until men we are;
> We believe in our Führer,
> We live for our Führer,
> We die for our Führer,
>   Until heroes we are.[68]

The myth of 'sacrifice' in speeches and ceremonies, and contained in these songs, became a major component of fascist mythology. J. P. Stern argues that the myth involves

> each writer 'sacrificing' himself for the common good of the Party, or of the Nation, for the Führer who in turn sacrifices himself for his *Volksgenossen*; everybody is ready to die for everybody else; the party and its programme are authenticated by promises not of benefits but of more and more sacrifices . . . The idea of 'sacrifice' may be primitive enough (the point doesn't need arguing that there is nothing wrong with sacrifice and almost everything wrong with vaunting it); but as an all-purpose instrument of emotional blackmail, material extortion, and spiritual-religiose validation it cannot be improved on.[69]

The veneration of 'the heroic dead' thus figures as a major component of fascist ideology and the political rituals of fascist regimes. The body of the dead becomes the sacred body of a dead hero, giving rise to the cult of the dead in the most literal and obvious sense: the sanctification of the dead. If fascism is a political religion, as some believe, then the halo of 'sacredness' is emancipated from any religious content and taken over by secular and politically charged concepts such as the fallen soldier. At the same time, its most holy places are those where men have fought and died for the nation. As Rosenberg put it, 'sacred places are all those upon which German heroes have died for these ideas. Sacred are those places where memorial stones and monuments remember them.'[70]

But note the important slippage that has begun to take place in the last few paragraphs, from sacrifice for the nation (as exemplified by the war dead) to sacrifice for the fascist movement and regime. Fascism's expertise at ideologically obliterating the differences between groups, forces and powers (there are no class divisions, the Party is the people, the leader is the state and so on), combined with the fact that many of those returning from the war became members of the Freikorps in Germany and the Arditi del Popolo in Italy, which in turn were integral to the final triumph of fascism, meant that the sanctification of the 'war dead' was easily turned into the sanctification of those who died for the movement. The fallen of Langemarck merged with the martyrs of the Felderrnhalle, the cult of the fallen soldier was transformed into the cult of the fallen fascist and the Unknown Soldier became the Unknown SA man. Thus when individual 'heroes' were singled out they were often heroes in both the military (First World War) and political (fascist) senses. Those who died in the cause of fascism were increasingly buried in cemeteries for the war dead, and Mussolini came to describe dead fascist activists as 'the latest to fall in the Great war'.[71]

On this basis the regimes in both Germany and Italy introduced a range of paraphernalia concerning the dead of the movement, from the *squadrista* emblem of a skull with dagger between the teeth and the *Totenkopfring* (Death's Head Ring) worn by the SS, to far more elaborate and public shrines and exhibitions to commemorate dead heroes.[72] The regime in Italy produced *I caduti della milizia* (The Fallen of the Milizia) (1932) offering biographies of 370 Black Shirts who 'had fallen for the Fascist Revolution' between 1923 and 1931. Every branch party kept a shrine, pennons of fascist groups were named after the fallen, and new works or classrooms in schools were often dedicated to the memory of fallen heroes. (The colour black was

also chosen in part because of its association with death: 'Black shirt
or black flag/the colour of death', the Arditi used to sing.[73]) The 1932
Exhibition of the Fascist Revolution to celebrate ten years of fascist
rule in Italy contained a 'Gallery of Fasci' dedicated to the *fasci di
combattimento*, and a hall dedicated to the martyrs of the fascist
revolution, the 'Martyrs Sanctuary', universally acknowledged to be
the masterpiece and focal point of the exhibition. Hitler commissioned Königsplatz tombs to hold the party martyrs, drew up plans
for a gigantic Soldiers Hall in Berlin to honour dead heroes, a
mausoleum and two 'cemeteries of honour'. In addition the Nazis also
planned a network of gigantic *Totenburgen*, citadels to the dead, to be
placed at key battle sites across the empire.

   This notion of sacrificial death was also important to the
ideological interpellation of women. Mussolini, for example,
encouraged women to attend the cemeteries to honour the war dead,
and to participate in the 'Day of the Wedding Rings' (1935) in which
the fascists collected hundreds of thousands of gold wedding rings
from women in exchange for iron rings from the Duce in a mystic
marriage under the sign of Birth and Death. Mussolini also invented
the female 'death squadron', which included widows and mothers in
mourning or semi-mourning, and devised a black uniform with a skull
on the breast for the women squadron members who attacked 'the
reds'. Mussolini's speeches to women from 1936 to 1941, in which he
referred to them as widows, mothers, sisters and daughters of dead
soldiers, were accompanied by a totally black scenic display and the
skull and crossbones which the fascists hoisted on their flags.[74] It was
coffins as much as cradles that occupied fascist speeches and writings
on the place of women.

   Tributes and references to the dead were thus present in nearly every
fascist ceremony. The dreary nod to 'traditional' folklore in activities
such as the dances around the Maypole, which commentators have
discussed time and again, were nothing compared to the impressive
displays invented to ecstatically celebrate and worship the dead.
Behind the pomp and circumstance of fascist spectacle, death always
stood waiting in the wings, ready to take centre stage.[75]

   On occasion key individuals became singled out for serious
adoration. Perhaps the most famous of these in Nazi Germany is
Horst Wessel.[76] For example, on 22 January 1933 – Horst Wessel
Memorial day – Goebbels staged a march of the Berlin SA to KPD
headquarters, despite (or perhaps because of) the likelihood of

violence. Thirty-five thousand SA men eventually made their way to Wessel's grave, where Hitler made the kind of speech common in the cult of the fallen hero:

> With his song, which is sung by millions today, Horst Wessel has erected a monument to himself in ongoing history which will last much longer than this stone and iron memorial . . . Comrades, raise the flags. Horst Wessel, who lies under this stone, is not dead. Every day and every hour his spirit is with us, marching in our ranks.[77]

But rather than focus on the well-known figure of Wessel, I want to say just a little about one other such hero, Albert Leo Schlageter. I do so as a way of broadening out the argument a little, through the incorporation of the more philosophical dimension to the fascist death-drive, as found in the work of Martin Heidegger. This will then lead to the crux of the argument in this chapter, concerning im-mortality and resurrection.

Schlageter had fought in the war, apparently with extreme bravery, and was eventually promoted to lieutenant and awarded the Iron Cross First and Second Class. A short spell at Freiburg University following the war only served to increase his sense of frustration at the post-war political settlement, and so he quickly joined the Freikorps. As a member of the Freikorps, Schlageter was deployed in the campaign against the Bolsheviks in the Baltic, 'liberating' Riga in May 1919, engaging in bloody class warfare at Bottrop in 1920, and supporting the Lithuanians in their struggle with Poland. In 1921, as a member of the Spezialpolizei, he took part in a range of undercover operations such as penetrating the Polish underground. In Berlin in 1922 he joined the Nazi party, and during 1923 spent much of his time trying to subvert the French control of the Ruhr region, including dynamiting railway lines to stop the transport of German coal to France. Following one such dynamiting operation, Schlageter was arrested by the French, tried by a military court, sentenced to death and executed on 26 May 1923.

Following his death Schlageter became a hero for the German right. On the morning of Schlageter's burial a crowd of around 25,000 came to hear a eulogy for him in Munich given by Adolf Hitler. The day after Schlageter had been shot the Schlageter-Gedächtnis-Bund was founded in Hanover. The Bund's central office was closely allied with National Socialism, in terms of membership, ideology, use of symbols and, not least, a desire to glorify dead heroes. More generally, Schlageter became a popular subject of heroic music, the songs of which focused on his death – 'he died for us, Schlageter, first hero of liberty'. On the first anniversary of his death countless memorial services took place, including one at his graveside, which sought to conjure up the spirit of the dead hero. A sample speech runs: 'You have redeemed us like that other hero who died on the cross at Golgotha, and you have given us the strength to live and to die just as you did, for your belief in freedom and greatness for our Volk and Fatherland. Albert Leo Schlageter lives!'[78] The high point of this glorification of the life and death of Schlageter was the Schlageter National Memorial, unveiled in 1931 amid great pomp and attended by notables from the political and business world. The Memorial itself

> was an architectural triumph, a felicitous union of landscape, form, and function. Instead of a swastika, a striking Christian Cross of iron towered over the hearth where he died, suggestive of the promise of resurrection. At the base of the monument, the name Albert Leo Schlageter was inscribed, inviting visitors into an unadorned marble crypt, which lay very low to the ground. There one found the names of all those who had died in the battle for the Ruhr.[79]

Throughout the 1920s the Nazis had sought to control the Schlageter legacy. In *Mein Kampf*, for example, Schlageter's name appears at the very beginning of the text, just after the dedication to those who died at the Felderrnhalle.[80] It took little effort to control the legacy fully after the seizure of power. The tenth anniversary of Schlageter's death in 1933 coincided with the Nazi seizure of power, and 20 April that year saw the premier of Hanns Johst's play *Schlageter*, featuring many well-known actors, at the official state theatre in Berlin, and dedicated to Hitler (on his birthday). Unsurprisingly, the play functioned as praise for both National Socialism and Schlageter, who of course emerges as a good Nazi as well as a good German; audiences reached 35,000 in 1935 and 80,000 in 1943. Countless other commemorations took place that first year of power, including one in Düsseldorf that lasted three days. By the end of 1933 Schlageter had been declared the first National Socialist German soldier and thereby took his place alongside Horst Wessel as a cult figure.

All in all, then, Schlageter was easily incorporated into the pantheon of Nazi heroes; as such, there might not be much else to say. But one of the memorials, held on 26 May 1933, was at Freiburg University, and one of the speakers there was Martin Heidegger. Heidegger had already had quite a busy month, having been appointed as rector of the University on 21 April and having joined the Nazi Party on 1 May. Heidegger's speech at the programmatic rectorship address held on 27 May, 'Die Selbstbehauptung der Deutschen Universität' (The Self-Assertion of the German University) has been the focus of much of the debate about Heidegger's ideological affiliations with National Socialism. But actually, one can learn a lot about these affiliations and, conversely, learn a lot about fascism, by considering Heidegger's speech at the memorial service for Schlageter the day before.[81]

In his speech Heidegger speaks of Schlageter in terms which on one level are similar to those used in all the other speeches about him. 'Let us honor him by reflecting, for a moment, upon his death'; 'With a hard will and a clear heart, Albert Leo Schlageter died his death'; 'Student of Freiburg, let the strength of this hero's native mountains flow into your will'; and so on. At the final words, 'we honor the hero and raise our arms in silent greeting', the thousand or so present in the crowd raised their arms in silent memory. In many other ways Heidegger's speech is also continuous with National Socialist aims regarding Schlageter. He makes no mention of Schlageter's religious motivations, for example, which suited the character of the event organized by a section of the Nazis that excluded any connection with Catholic groups. But beyond these points, Heidegger's speech also had a far more systematic political and philosophical meaning, because at critical points it followed the lines of the analytic of Dasein in *Being and Time*.

The existential analysis of death in *Being and Time* is founded on the assumption of Dasein's totality, and the idea that 'the Being of this wholeness itself must be conceived as an existential phenomenon of a Dasein which is in each case one's own'.[82] As much as this gives self-preservation a key ontological position in the analysis of existence, so death also becomes centrally important, ultimately determining Heidegger's conception of Dasein:

> By its very essence, death is in every case mine, in so far as it 'is' at all. And indeed death signifies a peculiar possibility-of-Being in which the very Being of one's own Dasein is an issue . . . With death, Dasein stands before itself in its ownmost potentiality-for-Being.[83]

Death thus becomes the constitutive element of Dasein and thus the key to the ontology of *Being and Time*. This *Being-towards-death* means that

> *death, as the end of Dasein, is Dasein's ownmost possibility – non-relational, certain and as such indefinite, not to be outstripped. Death is, as Dasein's* end, in the Being of this entity *towards* its end . . . The problem of the possible Being-a-whole of that entity which each of us is, is a correct one if care, as Dasein's basic state, is 'connected' with death – the uttermost possibility for that entity.[84]

In his eagerness to push the idea of death as the ontological foundation of totality, Heidegger distinguishes authentic death from death as an everyday event subject to the 'idle talk' of 'the They'.

> The 'they' have already stowed away an interpretation for this event . . . The expression 'one dies' spreads abroad the opinion that what gets reached, as it were, by death, is the 'they' . . . 'Dying' is levelled off to an occurrence which reaches Dasein, to be sure, but belongs to nobody in particular.

But since Heidegger wants to present death as Dasein's ownmost possibility, it must 'become manifest to Dasein that in this distinctive possibility of its own self, it has been wrenched away from the "they". This means that in anticipation any Dasein can have wrenched itself away from the "they" already.' Saved from the '*constant tranquillization* about death' provided by the They, death becomes authentic. Heidegger summarizes the characterization of authentic Being-towards-death thus: 'anticipation reveals to Dasein its lostness in the they-self, and brings it face to face with the possibility of being itself, primarily unsupported by concernful solicitude, but of being itself, rather, in an impassioned *freedom towards death*'.[85]

In the short speech Heidegger comments several times that Schlageter 'died the most difficult and the greatest death of all'. He 'died the *most difficult* of all deaths. Not in the front line as the leader of his field artillery battery, not in the tumult of an attack, and not in a grim defensive action – no, he stood *defenseless* before the French rifles.' And so, Heidegger goes on, in his most difficult hour, he had also to achieve *the greatest thing of which man is capable*. Alone, drawing on his own inner strength, he had to place before his soul an image of the future awakening of the Volk to honor and greatness so that he could die believing in this future.

In the terms of *Being and Time*, Schlageter's death was 'non-relational, certain and as such indefinite, not to be outstripped'. The historically contingent circumstances which led Schlageter to his execution and the actual historical characteristics of Schlageter as a person – post-war alienation and political disaffection leading to membership of the volunteer corps – is ignored in favour of an ahistorical existential conception of pseudo-political compulsion: Schlageter *had to* achieve the greatest thing; he *had to* place a certain image before his soul; he was *compelled* to go to the Ruhr, *compelled* to go to the Baltic, *compelled* to go to Upper Silesia.[86] (And note that the places to which he had to go – the Baltic, Upper Silesia, the Ruhr – are the places in which the volunteer corps were most active.[87]) In other words, he *had to* die.

In political existentialism everything becomes focused on the most extreme 'crisis': the 'state of exception', 'the emergency situation' or, more broadly, death.[88] To the extent that Heidegger's philosophy can be described as a form of political existentialism, it has to be said that Heidegger participates in nothing less than the cult of death, engaging in a philosophical strategy that is inherently fascist. Victor Farías claims that Heidegger saw personified in Schlageter's death the fate of the German people following the end of the First World War and that 'this accords with the polemic of the extreme right and especially of the National Socialists'.[89] This is undoubtedly the case. But there is more to the story than the question of individual sacrifice and national standing. The references to the mountains and valleys of the Black Forest which helped shape Schlageter's 'clarity of heart' and 'harden his will' show a significant development of the argument in *Being and Time*. Where in *Being and Time* Dasein exists for-itself in 'the world' (*Welt*), the Schlageter speech (and other speeches) of 1933 has a far less abstract concept of space: it is the 'mountains, forests, and valleys of [the] Black Forest, the home of this hero'.[90] The references to the common homeland and a common origin were not just a way of registering with the listeners but also became, for Heidegger and fascism, the fundamental *raison d'être* of death. Only in dying for his 'homeland' and the German people could Schlageter act out a death that is non-relational, certain and as such indefinite – not to be outstripped. Schlageter's individual death is in the speech presented anew in terms of the collective future of Germany and as an example for German youth. The basis of Schlageter's ambitions was 'the greatness of the awakening nation' and the 'future awakening of the Volk'. He therefore died 'for the German people and its Reich'. Or as Heidegger was to put it in another speech a year later about those who had sacrificed themselves: 'Our comrades died an early death; this early death was, however, the most beautiful and greatest death. The greatest death because it dared to be the most supreme sacrifice for the fate (*Schicksal*) of the Volk.'[91] Writing just after the war, Karl Löwith commented that 'none of us could have anticipated in 1927, when Heidegger's *Being and Time* appeared, that six years later the death which is "always one's own" and which radically individuates, could be refashioned so as to herald the fame of a National Socialist hero'.[92] But of course the point is that the analysis of individual death in *Being and Time* – although as we have seen even at this level it is nonetheless complicit with the fascist claptrap concerning death – shifts in the speech on Schlageter to a Dasein which oscillates between universality and the particular political collective of a German Dasein. Thus 'freedom towards death' becomes, within the horizon of popular community, the sacrifice of one's life for the nation. The violence inherent in Heidegger's philosophy is thus a violence that lies in the constellation of forces which unite *collective* Being and death.[93]

For fascism, then, the cult of the fallen soldier and the memory of the dead went far beyond commemoration; rather, it became a philosophy of life. 'Death *is*', says Heidegger; 'Long Live Death!', cry the fascist activists. And with this phrase we are at the core of fascist theory and practice – both past and present.[94] But this begs the question: what does it mean?

It would be easy to take the slogan at face value: if nothing else it explains why fascists seem to like killing lots of people. Contemporary fascists (or, as they tend to prefer, 'racial nationalists' or 'revolutionary nationalists') insist that the slogan 'is not the advocacy of genocide'. Rather, they claim, 'it is the fraternal salute, the greeting which acknowledges that Revolutionary Nationalists are prepared to sacrifice all in service of their noble cause'.[95] A comment made by Goebbels is telling on this score. Speaking at the funeral of Nazi hero Hans Maikowski on 5 February 1933, just days after the seizure of power and in the presence of some 40,000 SS, SA and Hitler Youth, Goebbels commented:

here we stand at his open grave, and this proverb surely fits the one we are about to return to the bosom of mother earth: Perhaps we Germans don't know much about living, but as for death – that we do fabulously! This young man knew how to die, this he could do fabulously.[96]

Likewise, Mussolini and Gentile comment that the most important element in the rise of fascism was that it preferred action and battle to research and debate: 'discussions there were, but something more sacred and more important was occurring: death. Fascists knew how to die.'[97] So maybe, if the fascists are right, the slogan is about nothing other than knowing how to sacrifice one's life for the nation – dying fabulously – and we should leave it at that.

But maybe there is more to be said. What I aim to tease out from the slogan is the inherent identification of fascism and death. Not 'real' or 'everyday' death and its mundane but individually tragic banality, but death in its most political and aestheticized form. Attempts to compare fascism with other forms of genocide in terms of a 'death count' – the Holocaust compared to the Gulag, X million compared to Y million dead and so on – miss this point of the centrality of death to fascism; they miss, in other words, part of its qualitative specificity. But this specificity lies not just in the fact that fascism constitutes a movement geared towards the production of a society which has the death camp as its greatest achievement. It lies also in the fact that an *active embrace of death* is core to the theory and practice of the movement. This active embrace is about much more than just sacrifice. Rather, it rests on the assumption that *the dead are never really dead* and, as such, the belief that the dead can be made to once again fight the battle.[98] What I aim to tease out, in other words, is what makes resurrection one of fascism's central categories, and the danse macabre its greatest pleasure.

Resurrection; or the danse macabre

The term 'Long Live Death!' came to be used by nationalist groups in Europe between the First and Second World Wars. It was made famous by D'Annunzio's legionnaires and adopted by the Italian Arditti, but became better known in the context of the Spanish Civil War. 'Viva la Muerte!' was a favorite motto of General Millán Astray of the Spanish Falange. In a confrontation between Miguel de Unamuno and Millán

Astray at the University of Salamanca in October 1936 one of the
General's followers is reported to have shouted the slogan from the
back of the hall during a speech by Unamuno. Unamuno is reported to
have said:

> Just now I heard a necrophilious and senseless cry: 'Long live death!' . . . I
> must tell you, as an expert authority, that this outlandish paradox is
> repellent to me . . . This is the temple of the intellect. And I am its high
> priest . . . You will win, because you have more than enough brute force. But
> you will not convince. For to convince you need to persuade. And in order
> to persuade you would need what you lack: Reason and Right.[99]

During the last comments Millán Astray is said to have shouted in
reply: 'Death to intelligence! And long live Death!' In a nice touch
illustrating that he was as interested in the practice as well as the
theory behind the slogan, he ordered Unamuno out of the University
at gunpoint.

We might note that the confrontation encapsulates the nature of
fascism's essentially irrationalist response to 'rationalist' political
doctrines such as liberalism and Marxism, but that is not my concern
here. My interest, rather, is in Unamuno's suggestion that the cry is
necrophilious. Out of this suggestion and the kind of cult of death I
have been discussing, Erich Fromm has argued that fascism is a
necrophiliac phenomenon driven by necrophilious leaders and
maintained by necrophilious followers. The destructive tendency within
fascism and described by most commentators is, for Fromm, part of a
'passionate attraction to all that is dead, decayed, putrid, sickly'. It is
'the passion to transform that which is alive into something unalive; to
destroy for the sake of destruction . . . It is the passion to tear apart
living structures.'[100] Conversely, Elias Canetti has argued that at the
heart of mass politics is the question of survival; the dead are thus
important symbolically. 'In the eyes of those who are still alive
everyone who is dead has suffered a defeat, which consists in *having
been survived*.'[101] The sense of defeat experienced by the dead is
matched by the feeling of 'superiority' felt by the survivors, a feeling
most marked in those who fought in war. 'Simply because he is still
there, the survivor feels that he is *better* than they [the dead] are. He
has proved himself, for he is alive. He has proved himself among many
others, for the fallen are not alive.'[102] Thus the 'accumulation of
experiences of other people's deaths is, I believe, one of the essential

seeds of power'.[103] Theweleit has applied this argument to fascism, suggesting that

> it is not corpses that this man [Hitler, but the point stands for fascists in general] loves; he loves his own life. But he loves it . . . for its ability to survive. Corpses piled upon corpses reveal him as a victor, a man who has successfully externalized that which is dead within him, who remains standing when all else is crumbling.[104]

There is some strength in this argument, although it might be accused of suffering from the same ahistorical characterological definitions which weaken Fromm's account.

In contrast to both Fromm's argument and Theweleit's reading of Canetti, it has also been argued that fascism's destructive tendency means that it is driven towards neither the love of death nor the accumulation of the experience of death, but to its *own* destruction: 'the final programme for Germany was national death . . . Hitler condemned Germany to national death.'[105] As Albert Speer comments following his own part 'inside the Third Reich', Nazism's final swansong was the death sentence of the German people.[106] Fascism in this sense can be read as an ideology of suicide, and the fascist state a suicide state. Foucault comments that 'the objective of the Nazi regime was . . . not really the destruction of other races. The destruction of other races was one aspect of the project, the other being to expose its own race to the absolute and universal threat of death.'[107] Accepting the likelihood of total destruction was thus central to the fascist project, which had to reach the point at which the entire population had to be exposed to death, as witnessed by the flurry of decrees from 19 March (the 'Nero Decree') and into early April 1945 in which Hitler appeared to order the destruction of Germany's infrastructure. The 'suicide epidemic' of February to May 1945 (in which several thousand Germans took their own lives) captures this well, but Hitler's decision to blow out his own brains is surely the highpoint of this 'suicidal tendency' – the suicide of the leader as emblematic of the suicide state. Gilles Deleuze and Félix Guattari thus claim that:

> In fascism, the State is far less totalitarian than it is *suicidal*. There is in fascism a realized nihilism. Unlike the totalitarian State, which does its utmost to seal all possible lines of flight, fascism is constructed on an

intense line of flight, which it transforms into a line of pure destruction and abolition. It is curious that from the very beginning the Nazis announced to Germany what they were bringing: at once wedding bells and death, including their own death, and the death of the Germans. They thought that they would perish but that their undertaking would be resumed, all across Europe, all over the world, throughout the solar system. And the people cheered, not because they did not understand, but because they wanted that death through the death of others . . . Suicide is presented not as a punishment but as the crowning glory of the death of others. One can always say that it is not just a matter of foggy talk and ideology, nothing but ideology. But that is not true. The insufficiency of economic and political definitions of fascism does not simply imply a need to tack on vague, so-called ideological determinations. [Thus] Nazi statements . . . always contain the 'stupid and repugnant' cry, *Long live death!*, even at the economic level, where the arms expansion replaces growth in consumption and where investment veers from the means of production toward the means of pure destruction.[108]

Foucault makes the point more starkly: 'we have an absolutely racist state, an absolutely murderous state, and an absolutely suicidal state . . . The three were necessarily superimposed.'[109]

Necrophiliac? Survivalist? Suicidal? These claims have an obvious appeal, offering a nice way of explaining the transformation of the blood myth into the blood bath and the mechanisms by which a whole society might become geared towards the production of corpses; it is surely much easier to legitimize mass murder when your slogan is 'Long Live Death!'. So in that sense 'necrophiliac', 'survivalist' and 'suicidal' seem to go some way to capture the idea of fascism as, in Jean Baudrillard's terms, 'an aesthetic perversion of politics, pushing the acceptance of a culture of death to the point of jubilation'.[110]

But – and it is an enormous but – this is not quite enough. There is a sense in which these interpretations are just a little too neat. For all their purported radicalism, they offer a rather easy interpretive option, for taken either together or individually the interpretations encourage us to box fascism into the corner marked 'death' and leave it at that. Yet just as we saw that it is not so easy for Marxism to let the dead bury their dead, so we find that the reading of fascism as either necrophilious or suicidal has major problems. Identifying these problems will help us make sense of the importance of the dead to fascism and to tease out some of the ways this is distinguishable from Marxism as discussed in the previous chapter.

The problem with the idea of fascism as necrophiliac, survivalist or suicidal is one which takes us to the heart of the issue. That is that in many ways the fascist does not love death per se, so to speak. Rather, fascism thinks of the dead as in some sense either alive or as possessing the possibility of becoming alive once more. After all, 'one cannot escape this world entirely'.[111] Remember: 'Albert Leo Schlageter lives!' And recall Hitler's speech on Horst Wessel Memorial Day: 'Horst Wessel . . . *is not dead*. Every day and every hour his spirit is with us, marching in our ranks.' Or as the obituary of Wessel in Goebbels's *Der Angriff* put it: 'The deceased who is with us, raises his weary hand and points into the dim distance: Advance over the graves! At the end lies Germany!'[112] This same point was made time and again by leading figures. At the 1935 commemoration for those who died at the Felderrnhalle Hitler commented that they are an example because '*for us they are not dead*', adding: 'Long live our Volk! And may today the dead of our Movement, Germany and its men, living and dead, live on!'[113]

Of course, the difficulty with suggesting that the dead are not dead is that they are clearly, on one level, really dead. The ideological solution to this is to present the dead as either *living* in the sense that they are *immortal* or as in the process of being *resurrected* as part of the greater future. Hence the comments on Wessel: 'his soul was resurrected, to live among us all' Hitler comments, adding the lines from the Horst Wessel song – 'he is marching in our ranks'; 'you [Wessel] had first to pale in death/before becoming immortal for us', SA poet Anacker adds.[114] *Mein Kampf* is a call not just to the German nation, but to the German dead – a call for the resurrection not just of the nation, but of the dead themselves. The first step towards the 'nationalization of the masses' is 'to win the masses for a national resurrection': 'without the clearest knowledge of the racial problem and hence of the Jewish problem there will never be a resurrection of the German nation'. Not a 'mechanical restoration of the past', but 'the resurrection of our people'.[115] The dead are not going to take this insult – of German defeat and the post-war settlement (but maybe also of being treated as 'dead'?) – lying down, or even be restricted to turning in their graves. Rather, 'the spirits of the dead . . . quicken':

> Would not the graves of all the hundreds of thousands open, the graves of those who with faith in the fatherland had marched forth *never to return*? Would they not open and send the silent mud- and blood-covered heroes

back as spirits of vengeance to the homeland which had cheated them with such a mockery?[116]

As Heidegger put it in 1934 (again eliding the difference between those killed in the Great War and those killed in the fight for Nazism):

> The Great War is only now coming upon us. The awakening of our dead, the two million dead from out of the endless graves . . . this awakening is only now beginning. The Great War is only today becoming for us Germans – and for us among all peoples – a historical reality of our Dasein, for history is not what has been, nor what is present. History is, rather, the futural and our mandate for this.[117]

Or as Hitler put it in his 1935 speech commemorating the Felderrn-halle dead:

> These sixteen soldiers have celebrated a resurrection unique in world history . . . They are now attaining German immortality. Back then [in 1923] they could not yet see today's Reich, but only sense its coming. Fate denied them the chance to personally witness this Reich. However, because they were no longer allowed to personally witness and see this Reich, we will make certain that this Reich sees them. And that is the reason why I have neither laid them in a vault nor banned them to some tomb . . . For us they are not dead. These pantheons are not vaults but an eternal guard-house. Here they stand guard for Germany and watch over our Volk . . . Long live our National Socialist Germany! Long live our Volk! And may today the dead of our Movement, Germany and its men, living and dead, live on![118]

The preparation for sacrifice noted above might thus be better understood as a preparation for *eternal life* rather than a preparation for death. This is, of course, a distinctly religious trope – and note Hitler's comment that 'a religion in the Aryan sense cannot be imagined which lacks the conviction of survival after death in some form'[119] – but it is important to note that what is being stressed in these comments, and therefore what needs to be the object of our attention, is a sense of immortality and/or resurrection.[120]

The belief in immortality or resurrection makes the idea of sacrifice a lot easier, since 'the more we suffer, the more glorious will be the resurrection of eternal Germany!'[121] Thus the SS could proclaim itself in 1937 to have 'grown within our newly resurrected people': 'we believe we will be not just the grandchildren who fought the fight more resolutely, but also the ancestors of later generations necessary for the eternal life of the German and Germanic people'.[122] This is the real theme of fascist songs.

> Ring, thou Bell of Revolution!
> Ring and call the fighting warriors,
> Call the graybeards, call the young men,
> Call the sleepers from their couches,
> Call the young girls from their chambers,
> Call the mothers from their cradles.
> Let the air be shrill with warning,
> With a warning of dire vengeance!
> Call the dead from mouldering grave vaults
> With a thunderous cry for vengeance.
> Vengeance! Vengeance!
> Germany Awake![123]

Now, calling girls from their chambers and mothers from their cradles is one thing; calling the dead from their grave vaults quite something else. But what is being stressed here is a *continuum* between life and death. This explains why the Nazis eventually came to *attack* the cult of the Unknown Soldier – on the grounds that the fallen were not dead at all but alive, and because faith in Nazi Germany united the fallen and the living. It also explains Maurice Barrès's myth of *debout les morts*, which told of dead soldiers coming to the aid of the living in battle, revived after the war in texts such as Henri Bonnet's *Almanach du Combattant* (1922) and Roland Dorgelès's *Le Reveil des Morts* (1923) aiming to show that the fallen were not really dead and to argue that, given their sacrifice, they should be consulted about the future of France.[124]

For fascism, the process of commemoration is not just about memory, but about *immortalizing* the dead in some kind of *occult time* uniting past, present and future (and therefore in stark contrast to the historical futurity of Marxism). 'Commemoration', Mussolini comments, 'means entering into the community of souls that binds the living and the dead.'[125] Part of the state's function as a sacred entity which is 'not only present, but past, and, above all, future', is thus, in Mussolini's words, to 'immortalize the names of those who died to defend its integrity'.[126] As one Langemarck veteran was to write in 1935, 'the graves of Langemarck glow with a new heavenly light. *The*

dead have returned home in us.'[127] Theodor Abel has shown the extent
to which the poem 'Victory' by Franz Lüdtke, with its insistence that
'we are the German immortality' was incredibly popular among
members of the Nazi movement.[128] The choir of Hitler Youth on
memorial day proclaimed 'the best of our people did not die that the
living might die, but that the dead might come alive'.[129] Thus when
Josef Magnus Wehner praises the dead of Langemarck, as seen above,
it is to show that the dead are not dead:

> The dying sang! The stormers sang. The young students sang as they were
> being annihilated: 'Deutschland, Deutschland über alles, über alles in der
> Welt'. But by singing this song, they were resurrected once more, a thousand
> times, and they will rise again a thousand times until the end of the Reich.

Although dead, the faces of the heroes of Langemarck show nothing
but 'the eternal happiness of the immortal . . . They are more alive than
we.'[130]

These ideas have a strong overlap in the sense that the dead are not
dead precisely because they are immortal. Their immortality allows
them their resurrection, but their resurrection shows that they are not
dead. This overlap is yet another example of fascism being able to
operate with seemingly contradictory ideas, or at least reveals fascism's
unwillingness to work systematically through any tensions between
key ideological presuppositions. It is important, nevertheless, to
recognize the importance of these ideas to fascist ideology. For the
dead, on this view, are somehow present. Or rather: 'PRESENT!' The
aforementioned *I caduti della milizia* opens with an invocation to
the fascist dead that clearly thinks of them as not dead: 'make me
always more worthy of our Dead so that they themselves . . . respond
to the living: PRESENT!'[131] Similarly, on the stepped white marble
architrave of the ossuary at the most grandiose of the final burial sites
for the Italian war dead (at Redipuglia, where over 100,000 bodies
were eventually buried), the word 'PRESENT' was carved over and
over again in a kind of roll call of the dead. Funerals of fascists killed
in action also played on this idea of their continued presence. As
Emilio Gentile points out, the culminating moment of the funeral
ceremony was the roll call in which 'one of the leaders of the squad
would call out the dead man's name, and the crowd, on its knees,
bellowed 'Present!'.[132] Above the names of dead heroes in the 'Martyrs
Sanctuary' at the 1932 Exhibition of the Fascist Revolution in Italy the

word PRESENT! was repeated, and a metal cross was inscribed with the phrase 'per la patria immortale!' (For the Immortal Fatherland!)

This idea of the presence of the dead was a perennial theme in Hitler's speeches commemorating the Feldherrnhalle dead: 'they too are present in spirit in our ranks, and in eternity they will know that their fight was not in vain', he comments in November 1934.[133] Joachim Fest describes the ceremony held by the Nazis one year later, again commemorating the Feldherrnhalle dead:

> The architect Ludwig Troost had designed two classicistic temples for Munich's Königsplatz; these were to receive the exhumed bones, now deposited in sixteen bronze sarcophagi, of the first 'martyrs' of the Nazi movement. The night before, during the traditional Hitler speech in the Bürgerbräukeller, the coffins had been placed on biers in the Feldherrnhalle, which was decorated with brown drapes and flaming braziers for the occasion . . . With raised arm, Hitler ascended the red-carpeted stair. He paused before each of the coffins for a 'mute dialogue'. Six thousand uniformed followers, carrying countless flags and all the standards of the party formations, then filed silently past the dead. On the following morning, in the subdued light of a November day, the memorial procession began. Hundreds of masts had been set up with dark red pennants bearing the names of the 'fallen of the movement' inscribed in golden letters. Loudspeakers broadcast the Horst Wessel song, until the procession reached one of the offering bowls, at which the names of the dead were called out . . . Then solemn silence descended while Hitler laid a gigantic wreath at the memorial tablet. While 'Deutschland, Deutschland über Alles' was played at a mournful tempo, all began to move toward Königsplatz down a lane of thousands upon thousands of flags dipped in salute to the dead. United in the 'March of Victory', the names of the fallen were read out in a 'last roll call'. The crowd answered 'PRESENT!' on their behalf. Thus the dead took their places in the 'eternal guard'.[134]

The 'presence' of the dead explains why we 'raise our arms in silent greeting' (Heidegger, greeting Schlageter), for these processions and commemorations are fascist rallies of a particular kind: they are rallies of the undead, taking place in some indeterminate other world, where history's victims are forever present to each other.[135]

In other words, what motivates and mobilizes fascism is less necrophilia or suicide and more a desire to communicate with and on behalf of, and in that sense to resurrect, the dead. Fascists are never more at home than when communing with the dead, acting as if the

dead are immortal and thus somehow *present*. This is Heidegger's
point about the need to *be with* the dead.

> In tarrying alongside him [the dead] in their mourning and com-
> memoration, those who have remained behind *are with him* . . . In such
> Being-with the dead [dem Toten], the deceased *himself* is no longer
> factically 'there'. However . . . those who remain can still *be with him*.[136]

Schlageter, and the dead, live on.

It is this desire to communicate with, to resurrect, and to be with
the dead that partly explains the interest in the occult in the fascist,
and especially the Nazi, tradition.[137] While biographies of Hitler
frequently trace his arguments regarding race to 'respectable' thinkers
such as Gobineau, Nietzsche, Wagner and Chamberlain, it is more
likely that he would have picked up ideas to rationalize his own
outlook and politics from cheap and accessible pamphlets in Vienna
such as *Ostara*, the racist-occult magazine run by Jörg Lanz von
Liebenfels, the main idea of which was that there existed an evil race
whose blood and genes were slowly dispossessing the German
people.[138] We know that in his politically formative years Hitler was
fascinated by the occult: his small collection of books as a student
contained works on mythology and a collection of *Ostara*; and despite
his later scepticism about Teutonic cults, Hitler's friends also recalled
many conversations on occult themes. While Hitler himself eventually
came to distance himself from such connections, key fascists such as
Walther Darré and Heinrich Himmler continued to peddle the 'sinister
runic nonsense' (as Walter Benjamin puts it),[139] and Nazism in general
has always kept 'one foot in the dark irrationalist world of Teutonic
myth, where heroic doom was regarded positively'.[140] An interest in
the occult continues to be almost *de rigueur* on the far right. However
'scientific' racism tries to be, it easily and nearly always slips into
mysticism and from there into occultism.[141] Ideologically this is hardly
surprising since, as Frederick Engels first pointed out, mysticism,
spiritualism and occultism are invariably ways of trying to undermine
the materialism of the communist tradition.[142]

It is for these reasons that esoteric and occult groups were also
crucial to the early organizational development of fascism in
Germany. The DAP had strong intellectual, political and membership
overlaps with the Thule Society (named after the supposedly legendary
homeland of the German race), led by Guido von List and Lanz

von Liebenfels and based on the theosophical currents of the time amalgamating Eastern philosophies and theosophy with a more mainstream anti-Semitism and anti-communism. One of the key figures in the Thule Society, Rudolf von Sebottendorff, published in late 1933 a book *Bevor Hitler Kam* (Before Hitler Came), the principal thesis of which was that Thule members were the people to whom Hitler first turned and who were crucial to the development of the National Socialist movement.[143] These overlaps continued as the DAP became the NSDAP.[144] The Thule also bestowed on the Nazis the sign of the swastika, a symbol first suggested to Hitler by Friedrich Krohn, 'a dentist from Starnberg' (as Hitler describes him in *Mein Kampf*), who was a member of the Thule Society (as Hitler does not mention in *Mein Kampf*),[145] an organization which had long understood the swastika's connections with occultism, theosophy and the usual mish-mash of Eastern belief. Perhaps most importantly, the Thule Society understood the swastika as connected with the dead and as quintes-sentially Gothic in its ahistoric assertion of collective forces.[146] But the real point to be made here is that those sympathetic to occult themes believe that through the occult one communicates with the dead.

This is best illustrated in the attempt by Himmler and his inner circle to communicate with the spirits of dead Teutons at Wewelsburg castle. Himmler acquired the castle in 1934 as a museum and SS officers college, coming under direct control of the Reichsführer-SS Personal Staff in 1935. It was also in 1935 that Himmler established with Darré the Ahnenerbe, an 'independent institute' but with 'official status' within the Reich with a mandate to research into Germanic prehistory and archaeology, becoming in 1940 a formal division of the SS. It was the Ahnenerbe whose collection of human skulls was described at Nuremberg.[147] The design, rituals and ceremonies of Wewelsburg are also telling. The ceremonial centre was the large domed circular room of the north tower of the castle, in which hung the coats-of-arms devised for dead SS-Gruppenführer. The Death's Head Rings of dead SS members were also kept here as a symbolic expression of their enduring community in an order supposedly transcending death. The vault of the tower was the 'Hall of the Slain', with a floor decorated with the Black Sun, an occult source of energy. In the wings of the castle, study-rooms were named and furnished after figures representing a 'nordic mythology' such as Widukind, King Heinrich and Henry the Lion, while in the dining hall Himmler and his inner circle would aim to engage in mystic communication with the dead Teutons.[148] Himmler was continually entering into contact with the 'great men' of the past, a ritual intended to instil into the SS the realization that they were members of a select elite order and the continuation of a long line – an *immortal* line – of German nobility, as well as to convince them of the correctness of one of their mottoes: 'to give death and to take it'.[149] On 2 July 1936, the thousandth anniversary of the death of King Heinrich I, Himmler visited the king's tomb in Quedlinburg Cathedral, despite the fact that the tomb was empty. A year later he had the bones of Heinrich taken to the tomb in a solemn procession, declaring that from then on the tomb was to be a sacred spot. At midnight on the anniversary of the king's death thereafter Himmler would commune silently with the king. When the German army was evacuating Naples, Himmler's main concern was that it should remember to bring with it the tomb of Conradin, the last Hohenstaufen King.[150] Himmler here offered an additional dimension to the ideological focus on death. Whereas the cult of the dead was often about the recent dead, for example in the First World War, Himmler aimed to commune with the ancient dead. But the difference hardly matters since the Teutons, like the recently fallen, are alive.

I am arguing, then, that for fascism the point is not so much to love or desire death (in either others or themselves). This is no doubt important – after all, fascism would be nothing without the corpses piled around its feet. Rather, I am arguing that the dead are either about to be resurrected or are immortal; either way, they are *not dead*. Death, like war, is for fascism the basis of renewal or rebirth: death is the crucial step on the road to resurrection, a form of resurrection of the mass, a means of achieving and exercising one's immortality. As Mussolini comments, *resurrection has to begin with the dead*.[151] Thus we might say that central to fascism's ideological achievement was to instil in the masses the idea of resurrection as part of the attempt to instil new life in a nation threatened by death. Death becomes the basis of (eternal) life, 'immortality' functions as a sort of propagandistic life insurance for mass society, and the return of the dead seen as the equivalent of the march from the battlefront back to the homeland – the basis of a new unity in an nation divided. 'Germany awake!' becomes a cry to the dead as well as the living – a demand for resurrection as well as political action. Better still: a demand for resurrection *as* political action. For fascism the dead shall – must – return; the dead are somehow *not dead* in the fascist imaginary. They are undead.[152]

Coda

To say that the dead are not dead, or that they are to be mobilized in pursuit of a radically different political future, takes us back to two themes as they have emerged through the previous chapters. In the first place, what is the difference between fascism's concept of resurrection, Marxism's idea of redemption and the principle of reconciliation? In the second place, there is the question of the monstrous.

It may appear that fascism's interest in the dead is close to an argument concerning redemption, of the kind developed in Chapter 2. Saul Friedländer, for example, comments that what distinguishes Nazi anti-Semitism from 'ordinary' anti-Semitism is that in emphasizing the mythic dimensions of the race and the sacredness of pure blood Nazi anti-Semitism can be thought of as redemptive. 'Whereas ordinary racial anti-Semitism is one element within a wider racist worldview, in redemptive anti-Semitism the struggle against the Jews is the dominant aspect of a worldview in which other racist themes are but secondary appendages.'[1] A number of other writers have written in a similar vein. James Rhodes tries to make sense of Nazism's eschatological dimensions through the idea of redemption, while Geoff Eley comments on the importance of the redemptive potential of radical-nationalist movements during the rise of fascism; Michael Burleigh also uses the idea of redemption in arguing for Nazism as a political religion.[2] But redemption is the wrong concept here. As discussed in Chapter 2, redemption has a complex of meanings: the action of freeing, delivering or restoring; the action of freeing a prisoner or slave by payment of ransoms; theologically, it refers to deliverance from sin. But resurrection has a different set of connotations. Referring to a process of individual and collective rebirth as part of a new era, resurrection points us to the importance of the dead to this fundamental historical and political process and, moreover, implies that the era in question will reunite the dead with the living; indeed, the new era is signalled by this very unity. The choice of the concept here is politically telling, and draws our attention to a fundamental aspect of the distinction between Marxism and fascism. Where 'redemption' was identified in the previous chapter as connoting the *hopes and struggles* of the dead, 'resurrection' points less to the hopes of the dead and more to *the dead themselves*.

As I argued in Chapter 2, for Marxism the revolutionary commitment which encourages us to let the dead bury their dead must be articulated from the standpoint of redemption: shot through with the redemptive dynamic which animates a large number of political movements and sustained by a class hatred which helps complete the work of history – a politics grounded on a historical futurity tempered by the image of redemption. If nothing else, such a standpoint would endeavour to make the dead safe from fascism. And it can now be seen how important this is, for it is now clear that one of fascism's goals is to resurrect the dead to their place in the immortal struggle between racially constituted nations. While fascism's account of the coming greatness of the nation may superficially appear to be a version of historical futurity, it is in fact a mystical and occult time in which the dead are resurrected to be reunited with the living. This, combined with the nihilism, anti-humanism and political existentialism which permeates fascism's concept of the dead, makes it unlike anything in Marx or Marxism. It also makes it unlike anything found in Burke or conservatism, where the orientation to the dead is part of a traditionalism aiming to reconcile generations and accommodate contradictory forces into the present.

It may also appear that all this talk about resurrection and immortality is just a comforting thought for fascists to come to terms with their own death or the reasons for their sacrifice. But actually the idea of the undead turns out to be deeply troubling for the fascist. For if the dead are still with us or due for return in an act of historical vengeance, then is this not also true of the dead enemy? In other words, if good fascists don't die, but remain immortal as part of an eternal struggle, then is this not true of communists, Jews, gypsies, and so on? After all, are they not also part of the eternal struggle? Remember that for all the talk about the *biological* basis of race, Hitler was still compelled to think of Jews as 'an abstract race of the mind', and to therefore note the obvious: 'a race of the mind is more solid, more durable than just a race, pure and simple'.[3] The enemy can thus also take the form of the undead. And of course the undead do not die, but go on adding new victims and multiplying their forces. A common story told about concentration camp guards and their victims is telling here.

It is often said that one of the things most hated by concentration camp guards was when a prisoner chose to commit suicide. In *The*

Inoperative Community Jean-Luc Nancy cites one concentration
camp prisoner as suggesting that prisoners often thought of killing
themselves, 'if only to force the SS to run up against the limit of the
dead object one will have become'.[4] Nancy thinks of this in the way
that most others probably think of it: killing themselves would be a
form of resistance for the prisoner because the guards would suffer the
worst frustration – one cannot discipline or torture a dead object. But,
in terms of the argument in this book, it might be argued that the
reason the SS found prisoners killing themselves so frustrating is more
because of the guards' understanding that the prisoners were not
really dead. In 'dying' they had 'escaped' and entered the realm of
the undead, from where they could continue the business of world
domination without this or that particular guard being able to interfere.

What fascism fears, it therefore seems, is that its 'dead' enemies
might also be undead. And, as such, do they not then possess one of
the key characteristics of monstrosity? They are *not properly dead*.
And this takes us back, finally, to a question raised in the Introduction
and Chapter 3 but never answered: why do fascists like desecrating
graves? Jewish law suggests that 'treating a corpse disrespectfully
implies a belief that death is final and irreversible'.[5] Such a view will
always miss the point of grave desecration, which is in fact a political
act of extreme importance to fascism far beyond mere 'symbolic
destruction'. For fascism fears that the death of the enemy is precisely
not final and irreversible. Again, the reason for grave desecration is
that for fascism the struggle against the enemy has to take place partly
on the terrain of the dead. Unable actually to engage in this struggle in
the world of the undead, the fascist is forced to the next best thing:
attack the grave. All of which serves to reinforce part of the argument
made in Chapter 2: until Marxism wins the battle against fascism –
which is no more than saying it must win the battle against capitalism –
not even the dead will be safe.

Notes

Introduction

1   John Berryman, '53', in *77 Dream Songs* (London: Faber & Faber, 1959).
2   Bram Stoker, *Dracula* (1897), ed. Maurice Hindle (Harmondsworth: Penguin, 1993), pp. 265–6.
3   This is a point about monstrosity noted by many. See, for example, David E. Musselwhite, *Partings Welded Together: Politics and Desire in the Nineteenth-Century English Novel* (London: Methuen, 1987), p. 69; Timothy Beal, *Religion and its Monsters* (London: Routledge, 2002), p. 10; Richard Kearney, *Strangers, Gods and Monsters: Interpreting Otherness* (London: Routledge, 2003), p. 120.
4   Elias Canetti, *Crowds and Power* (1960), trans. Carol Stewart (London: Victor Gollanz, 1962), p. 262; also see Miguel de Unamuno, *The Tragic Sense of Life* (1921) (London: Fontana, 1962), p. 56.
5   Catherine Merridale, *Night of Stone: Death and Memory in Twentieth-Century Russia* (New York: Penguin, 2000), p. 85.
6   Nationalism is of course unthinkable without the dead. As Katherine Verdery puts it, 'nationalisms are forms of ancestor cult, writ large enough to encompass localized kin-group affiliations and to incorporate into the notions of "ancestors", "brothers", and "heirs" people with whom our immediate blood ties are nil' – *The Political Lives of Dead Bodies: Reburial and Postsocialist Change* (New York: Columbia University Press, 1999), pp. 104–5. For an alternative geographical and thematic focus see Russ Castronovo, *Necro Citizenship: Death, Eroticism, and the Public Sphere in the Nineteenth-Century United States* (Durham, NC: Duke University Press, 2001). Also see John E. Seery, *Political Theory for Mortals: Shades of Justice, Images of Death* (Ithaca, NY: Cornell University Press, 1996), p. 165. In this book I eschew talking of nationalism and instead focus on the three traditions in question, though of course much of what is said about nationalism, such as Verdery's comment, is true of its most virulent form, namely fascism.
7   Theodor Adorno, *Aesthetic Theory* (1970), trans. C. Lenhardt (London: Routledge, 1984), p. 72.
8   Philippe Ariès, *Western Attitudes Towards Death: From the Middle Ages to the Present*, trans. Patricia M. Ranum (Baltimore: John Hopkins University Press, 1974), p. 25.
9   Mircea Eliade, *Occultism, Witchcraft and Cultural Fashions: Essays in*

Comparative Religions (Chicago: University of Chicago Press, 1976), pp. 41, 42.

10 Verdery, *Political Lives*, p. 42.

11 Slavoj i ek, *Looking Awry: An Introduction to Jacques Lacan through Popular Culture* (Cambridge, MA: MIT, 1992), p. 22.

12 Beal, *Religion and its Monsters*, p. 5. Mark Dorrian, 'Monstrosity today', *Artifice*, 15 (1996), 50; also 'On the monstrous and the grotesque', *Word and Image*, 16/3 (2000), 310–17, 312.

13 Joyce Carol Oates, ' "I had no other thrill or happiness" ', *New York Review* (24 March 1994), 52–9, 56.

14 Stanley Cavell, *The Claim of Reason: Wittgenstein, Skepticism, Morality, and Tragedy* (Oxford: Clarendon Press, 1979), p. 418.

15 Carl Schmitt, *The Leviathan in the State Theory of Thomas Hobbes: Meaning and Failure of a Political Symbol* (1938), trans. George Schwab and Erna Hilfstein (Westport, CT: Greenwood Press, 1996), pp. 26, 35.

16 Noël Carroll, *The Philosophy of Horror, or Paradoxes of the Heart* (London: Routledge, 1990), p. 201. Also see Edward J. Ingebretsen, *At Stake: Monsters and the Rhetoric of Fear in Public Culture* (Chicago: University of Chicago Press, 2001), p. 6.

17 In that sense I am building on my arguments concerning the role of insecurity in the fabrication of social order, in *The Fabrication of Social Order: A Critical Theory of Police Power* (London: Pluto, 2000).

18 Bram Dijkstra, *Evil Sisters: The Threat of Sexuality and the Cult of Manhood* (New York: Alfred A. Knopf, 1996), pp. 311, 434.

19 Mark Neocleous, *Imagining the State* (Maidenhead: Open University Press, 2003).

20 Brian Massumi, *A User's Guide to Capitalism and Schizophrenia: Deviations from Deleuze and Guattari* (Cambridge, MA: MIT Press, 1992), p. 8.

1 Burke: The Monstrous Multitude

1 Richard Payne Knight, *An Analytical Inquiry into the Principles of Taste*, 4th edition (London: T. Payne & J. White, 1808), p. 384.

2 Edmund Burke, 'Letter to Richard Burke', *c.*10 October 1789, in *The Correspondence of Edmund Burke*, vol. 6, ed. Alfred Cobban and Robert A. Smith (Cambridge: Cambridge University Press, 1967), p. 30.

3 Edmund Burke, *Reflections on the Revolution in France* (1790), ed. Conor Cruise O'Brien (Harmondsworth: Penguin, 1968), pp. 92, 124, 160, 308, 313, 333, 350. Conversely, he also suggests to his correspondent that 'from the general style of your late publications of all sorts, one would be led to believe that your clergy in France were a sort of monsters' (p. 251).

4   Edmund Burke, *Thoughts on the Cause of the Present Discontents* (1770), in *Select Works of Edmund Burke*, vol. 1 (Indianapolis: Liberty Fund, 1999), p. 115. He also comments there (p. 119) on the 'monstrous state of things in this constitution'.

5   Burke, *Reflections*, pp. 171, 218. Burke also comments (pp. 85, 181) on how the revolutionaries may imagine his own argument.

6   Cited in Conor Cruise O'Brien, *The Great Melody: A Thematic Biography of Edmund Burke* (London: Sinclair-Stevenson, 1992), p. 33. In the introduction to the book O'Brien comments that central to a proper understanding of Burke's work is what Vico called *Fantasia*, translated by Isaiah Berlin as 'imaginative insight'.

7   Cited in Peter Hughes, 'Originality and allusion in the writings of Edmund Burke', *Centrum*, 4/1 (1976), 32–43, 32.

8   Don Herzog, *Poisoning the Minds of the Lower Orders* (Princeton: Princeton University Press, 1998), p. 13.

9   Thomas Paine, *Rights of Man* (1791–2), ed. Henry Collins (Harmondsworth: Penguin, 1969), p. 81.

10   Edmund Burke, *Letters on a Regicide Peace: Select Works of Edmund Burke*, vol. 3 (Indianapolis: Liberty Fund, 1999), p. 123, emphasis added.

11   Burke, *Reflections*, p. 92; also p. 335.

12   Burke, 'Letter to the Earl of Charlemont', 9 August 1789, in *Correspondence*, vol. 6, p. 10.

13   Burke, 'Letter to Charles-Jean-François Depont', November 1789, in *Correspondence*, vol. 6, p. 41. This is the letter that Burke refers to in the prefatory page of the *Reflections* as having been 'written some time in the month of October 1789'. But since it responds to Depont's letter of 4 November this could hardly have been the case.

14   Burke, *Letters on a Regicide Peace*, pp. 138, 314.

15   Edmund Burke, *A Philosophical Enquiry into the Origins of our Ideas of the Sublime and the Beautiful* (1757), ed. James T. Boulton (Oxford: Basil Blackwell, 1987), p. 57.

16   Ibid., pp. 136, 160.

17   Ibid., pp. 57, 73, 136. The first person to point out how odd this argument is was Richard Payne Knight: 'If [Burke] had walked up St. James's Street without his breeches, it would have occasioned great and universal *astonishment*; and if he had, at the same time, carried a loaded blunderbuss in his hands, the astonishment would have been mixed with no small portion of *terror*: but I do not believe that the united effects of these two powerful passions would have produced any sentiment or sensation approaching to sublime' (*Analytical Inquiry*, pp. 383–4).

18   Burke, *Philosophical Enquiry*, p. 58.

19   Ibid., pp. 51, 91.

20   Ibid., p. 39; also pp. 51, 131.

21 Ibid., p. 64.
22 Tom Furniss, *Edmund Burke's Aesthetic Ideology: Language, Gender and Political Economy in Revolution* (Cambridge: Cambridge University Press, 1993), pp. 17–40.
23 Burke, *Philosophical Enquiry*, pp. 59, 67.
24 Burke, *Thoughts on the Cause of the Present Discontents*, p. 71.
25 Furniss, *Edmund Burke's Aesthetic Ideology*, pp. 119–20.
26 Burke, *Philosophical Enquiry*, pp. 61–2.
27 Burke, *Reflections*, pp. 117, 159, 161, 171, 174, 175, 205, 216, 226, 231, 240, 301. 'The condition of France at this moment was so frightful and horrible, that if a painter wished to portray a description of hell, he could not find so terrible a model, or a subject so pregnant with horror' – 'Speech, 11 April 1794', cited in Ronald Paulson, *Representations of Revolution (1789–1820)* (New Haven: Yale University Press, 1983), p. 66.
28 Burke, *Reflections*, p. 171.
29 Furniss, *Edmund Burke's Aesthetic Ideology*, pp. 3, 116.
30 Terry Eagleton, *Heathcliff and the Great Hunger* (London: Verso, 1995), p. 50.
31 Ronald Paulson, 'Burke's sublime and the representation of revolution', in Perez Zagorin (ed.), *Culture and Politics from Puritanism to the Enlightenment* (Berkeley: University of California Press, 1980), p. 250. Work on the links between Burke's aesthetic ideology and his politics is now extensive. As well as the works cited here, see Neal Wood, 'The aesthetic dimension of Burke's political thought', *Journal of British Studies*, 4/1 (1964), 41–64; Frances Ferguson, 'The sublime of Edmund Burke, or the bathos of experience', *Glyph*, 8 (1981), 62–78.
32 Burke, *Philosophical Enquiry*, pp. 59, 64, 144.
33 Burke, *Reflections*, pp. 121, 131, 182, 189, 194, 277, 327, 372. In 'A Letter to a Member of the National Assembly', May 1791, Burke compares despots governing by terror with the dominion of awe. See *Further Reflections on the Revolution in France*, ed. Daniel E. Ritchie (Indianapolis: Liberty Fund, 1992), p. 55.
34 Burke, *Reflections*, pp. 117, 161, 174, 249.
35 Ibid., p. 249.
36 Ibid., pp. 159, 205.
37 Ibid., p. 231.
38 Ibid., p. 237.
39 Ibid., p. 240.
40 Ibid., pp. 160, 171, 216, 301.
41 Frances Ferguson, 'Legislating the sublime', in Ralph Cohen (ed.), *Studies in Eighteenth-Century British Art and Aesthetics* (Berkeley: University of California Press, 1985), p. 136; Furniss, *Edmund Burke's Aesthetic Ideology*, p. 119; Paulson, *Representations of Revolution*, pp. 66, 71; W. J. T. Mitchell, *Iconology: Image, Text, Ideology* (Chicago: University of

Chicago Press, 1986), p. 131; Stephen K. White, *Edmund Burke: Modernity, Politics, and Aesthetics* (London: Sage, 1994), pp. 69, 74.

42 Burke, *Philosophical Enquiry*, pp. 37, 40, 46, 134, emphases added.

43 Burke, *Reflections*, p. 185.

44 Burke, 'Thoughts on French affairs', December 1791, in *Further Reflections*, p. 230; 'Letter to a Member of the National Assembly', p. 43.

45 Burke, *Letters on a Regicide Peace*, pp. 72, 104, 128, 345, 355.

46 Ibid., pp. 367–8.

47 Ibid., pp. 138, 216, 385; 'A Letter to a noble Lord', February 1796, in *Further Reflections*, p. 291; 'Thoughts and details on scarcity' (1795), in *Select Works of Edmund Burke: Miscellaneous Writings* (Indianapolis: Liberty Fund, 1999), p. 91. For cannibalism see *Letters on a Regicide Peace*, pp. 130, 166, and 'Letter to a noble Lord', p. 311. The comment on cannibalism picks up on the idea in the *Reflections*, p. 249.

48 Burke, 'Letter to a noble Lord', p. 291. For an alternative translation of the passage, and an alternative reading based on the question of disgust, see Linda M. G. Zerilli, *Signifying Woman: Culture and Chaos in Rousseau, Burke, and Mill* (Ithaca, NY: Cornell University Press, 1994), p. 92.

49 Burke, *Letters on a Regicide Peace*, pp. 207, 253, 254; 'Letter to a noble Lord', p. 312.

50 David B. Morris, 'Gothic sublimity', *New Literary History*, 16/2 (1985), 299–319; Frans De Bruyn, 'Edmund Burke's Gothic romance: the portrayal of Warren Hastings in Burke's writings and speeches on India', *Criticism*, 29/4 (1987), 415–38, 418; Paulson, 'Burke's sublime', p. 253; Mark Edmundson, *Nightmare on Main Street: Angels, Sadomasochism, and the Culture of Gothic* (Cambridge, MA: Harvard University Press, 1997), p. 18; R. J. Smith, *The Gothic Bequest: Medieval Institutions in British Thought, 1688–1863* (Cambridge: Cambridge University Press, 1987), p. 113; David Punter, *The Literature of Terror, Volume 1: The Gothic Tradition* (London: Longman, 1996), p. 39.

51 Eve Kosofsky Sedgwick, *The Coherence of Gothic Conventions* (New York: Methuen, 1986), p. 3.

52 Marquis de Sade, 'Reflections on the novel' (1800), in *The 120 Days of Sodom and Other Writings*, trans. Austryn Wainhouse and Richard Seaver (New York: Grove Press, 1966), p. 109.

53 Michel Foucault, *Society must be Defended: Lectures at the Collège de France, 1975–76*, trans. David Macey (London: Allen Lane, 2003), p. 212.

54 De Bruyn, 'Edmund Burke's Gothic romance', p. 417.

55 Punter, *Literature of Terror*, vol. 1, p. 54.

56 José B. Monleón, *A Specter is Haunting Europe: A Sociohistorical Approach to the Fantastic* (Princeton: Princeton University Press, 1990), p. 32; also see De Bruyn, 'Edmund Burke's Gothic romance', p. 421.

57 See for example Aristotle, *De Generatione Animalium*, trans. Arthur Platt,

in *The Works of Aristotle*, ed. J. A. Smith and W. Ross (Oxford: Clarendon Press, 1912), 767ᵇ–770ᵇ.

58 Georges Canguilhem, 'Monstrosity and the monstrous', *Diogenes*, 40 (1962), 27–42, 31; Michel Foucault, *Abnormal: Lectures at the Collège de France 1974–1975*, trans. Graham Burchell (London: Verso, 2003), pp. 55–65.

59 Peter Brooks, *Body Works: Objects of Desire in Modern Narrative* (Cambridge, MA: Harvard University Press, 1993), p. 218. The same point is made by many others. See, for example, Rosi Braidotti, 'Signs of wonder and traces of doubt: on teratology and embodied differences', in N. Lykke and R. Braidotti (eds), *Between Monsters, Goddesses and Cyborgs: Feminist Confrontations with Science, Medicine and Cyberspace* (London: Zed Books, 1996); Noël Carroll, *The Philosophy of Horror, or Paradoxes of the Heart* (London: Routledge, 1990), p. 194; Jeffrey Jerome Cohen, 'Monster culture (seven theses)', in Jeffrey Jerome Cohen (ed.), *Monster Theory* (Minneapolis: University of Minnesota Press, 1996), pp. 3–25; Donna J. Haraway, *Modest_Witness@Second_Millenium.FemaleMan©_ Meets_OncoMouse™* (London: Routledge, 1997), pp. 214–15; David E. Musselwhite, *Partings Welded Together: Politics and Desire in the Nineteenth-Century English Novel* (London: Methuen, 1987), p. 59; Margit Shildrick, *Embodying the Monster: Encounters with the Vulnerable Self* (London: Sage, 2002).

60 I have argued this at length in *The Fabrication of Social Order: A Critical Theory of Police Power* (London: Pluto Press, 2000).

61 I am building here on comments by Foucault, *Abnormal*, p. 73, though Foucault sees the point in terms of juridico–moral rather than socio-political conduct and, as such, fails to see the more explicitly political teratology that emerges at this point. Moreover, when he does come to consider political monsters in the revolutionary period, he does so in terms of key individuals such as Louis XVI and Marie-Antoinette rather than collective forces in the way that I am seeking to do with Burke. He makes one passing reference to the revolutionary people as monstrous (*Abnormal*, p. 98).

62 Slavoj Žižek, *Enjoy Your Symptom!: Jacques Lacan in Hollywood and Out* (London: Routledge, 2001), p. 134; 'When the phallus appears', October, 58 (1991), 45–68, 64.

63 Burke, *Reflections*, p. 372.

64 See Mark Neocleous, *Imagining the State* (Open University Press, 2003), pp. 8–38.

65 Canguilhem, 'Monstrosity', p. 36.

66 Burke, *Reflections*, pp. 92, 228. This is how Burke uses 'monstrous' in the *Philosophical Enquiry*: an animal will follow certain measures and proportions 'otherwise it would deviate from its proper species, and become in some sort monstrous' (p. 99).

67 Burke, *Letters on a Regicide Peace*, pp. 367–8.

68 Burke, *Reflections*, pp. 124, 152, 194, 282; 'Letter to a noble Lord',
    pp. 314–18. Chris Baldick, *In Frankenstein's Shadow: Myth, Monstrosity,
    and Nineteenth-Century Writing* (Oxford: Clarendon Press, 1987), p. 18.
69 Canguilhem, 'Monstrosity', p. 36.
70 As a side issue it might be noted that one collective candidate for the role
    of the monster might well have been the Jew. Anne Norton has argued that
    in his references to 'Old Jewry', 'Jews and jobbers', 'literary caballers' and
    the 'Hebrew brethren' of Lord George Gordon, Burke furnishes a
    profound and gratuitous anti-Semitic construction of the Jews. Be that as
    it may, the Jews do not figure in Burke's argument as the essence of the
    mob and thus essentially monstrous. The Jew will, however, figure in this
    way for one tendency within fascism, as I shall explore in Ch. 3. For
    Norton's argument see *Bloodrites of the Post-Structuralists: Word, Flesh
    and Revolution* (London: Routledge, 2002), pp. 71–4.
71 Burke, *Letters on a Regicide Peace*, p. 266.
72 Burke, *Philosophical Enquiry*, p. 136.
73 Terry Eagleton, *Ideology of the Aesthetic* (Oxford: Blackwell, 1990), p. 56.
74 Burke, *Thoughts on the Cause of the Present Discontents*, pp. 90, 111. In a
    major speech on economical reform in 1780 he also comments on the
    necessity 'to have a government within itself, capable of regulating the vast
    and often unruly multitude which composed and attended it' – 'Speech on
    the plan for economical reform', 11 February 1780, in *The Works of the
    Right Honourable Edmund Burke*, vol. 2 (London: John C. Nimmo, 1899),
    p. 304.
75 Burke, *Reflections*, p. 372.
76 Ibid., p. 279. In a letter to William Wyndham of 27 September 1789 Burke
    comments on 'the Mob of . . . constituents ready to Hang' the National
    Assembly should it 'deviate into moderation'. See *Correspondence*, vol. 6,
    p. 25.
77 Burke, *Reflections*, pp. 164–5.
78 Furniss, *Edmund Burke's Aesthetic Ideology*, p. 129; Ferguson, 'Legislating
    the sublime', p. 136.
79 Burke, *Reflections*, p. 179.
80 See, for example, Adam Smith, *Inquiry into the Nature and Causes of the
    Wealth of Nations* (1776), ed. R. H. Campbell, A. S. Skinner and W. B. Todd
    (Indianapolis: Liberty Fund, 1979), pp. 460, 779.
81 Burke, *Reflections*, p. 173; also see his letter to Sir John Scott, 11 January
    1796, in *Correspondence*, vol. 8, p. 370. For a sense of the variety of
    Burke's synonyms for 'swinish multitude' see Herzog, *Poisoning the
    Minds*, pp. 505–45. In 1831 *Blackwood's Edinburgh Magazine* would draw
    these themes together in discussing 'that many-mouthed Monster, the
    Swinish Multitude . . . pretending to be the People' – *Blackwood's Edinburgh
    Magazine*, 'L'Envoy', 29 (January 1831), 141.

[82] Christopher Hill, 'The many-headed monster' (1965), in Hill, *Change and Continuity in Seventeenth-Century England* (New Haven: Yale University Press, 1974), pp. 181–204; Peter Linebaugh and Marcus Rediker, *The Many-Headed Hydra: The Hidden History of the Revolutionary Atlantic* (London: Verso, 2000).

[83] Thomas Hobbes, *Leviathan* (1651), ed. Richard Tuck (Cambridge: Cambridge University Press, 1991), p. 128.

[84] Monleón, *A Specter is Haunting Europe*, p. 48.

[85] C. B. Macpherson, *Burke* (Oxford: Oxford University Press, 1980), pp. 64, 66.

[86] Karl Marx, 'Contribution to the critique of Hegel's philosophy of law: introduction', in Karl Marx and Frederick Engels, *Collected Works*, vol. 3 (London: Lawrence & Wishart, 1975), p. 187.

[87] Cited in François Flahault, *Malice* (1998), trans. Liz Heron (London: Verso, 2003), p. 44.

[88] This also in part explains the references to 'hair-dressers', 'working tallow-chandlers' and 'innumerable servile, degrading, unseemly, unmanly and often most unwholesome and pestiferous occupations, to which by the social economy so many wretches are inevitably doomed' – references to members of the working class without having to use this term (*Reflections*, pp. 138, 271).

[89] O'Brien, *Great Melody*, p. 395. Also here see Frans De Bruyn, *The Literary Genres of Edmund Burke: The Political Uses of Literary Form* (Oxford: Clarendon Press, 1996), pp. 168, 171–2.

[90] Sarah Benton, 'Monsters from the deep', *New Statesman* (19 October 1984), 10–11.

[91] Laura Mulvey, 'Changes: thoughts on myth, narrative and historical experience', *History Workshop Journal*, 23 (1987), 3–19, 5.

[92] Stephen King, *Danse Macabre* (London: Warner Books, 1993), pp. 55–6.

[93] Timothy K. Beal, *Religion and its Monsters* (London: Routledge, 2002), p. 33.

[94] Michael Moore, 'How to talk to your conservative brother-in-law', *Guardian Weekend* (4 October 2003), 22–30, 25. On the psychic trope of fear shared by conservatism and fascism see Jacqueline Rose, 'Margaret Thatcher and Ruth Ellis' (1987), in *Why War? Psychoanalysis, Politics, and the Return to Melanie Klein* (Oxford: Blackwell, 1993), pp. 62–3, 65. Entirely appropriately in terms of the politics of the right being discussed here, Rose's examples concern Thatcher's 'swamping' speech, her claims about the 'misty phantom of socialism', her concern for the 'frightened minority' and so on.

[95] Theodor Adorno and Max Horkheimer, *Dialectic of Englightenment* (1944), trans. John Cumming (London: Verso, 1979), p. 234.

[96] Burke, *Reflections*, pp. 105, 121, 124, 141, 143, 148, 247, 285, 375–6. On the forefathers also see pp. 119, 123.

97 Edmund Burke, 'Speech on moving tesolutions for conciliation with the colonies' (1775), in *Select Works of Edmund Burke* (Indianapolis: Liberty Fund, 1999), pp. 258–9.

98 Burke, *Reflections*, pp. 106, 117, 119, 122, 129, 142, 144, 276.

99 Ibid., p. 123; also see p. 353.

100 Ibid., pp. 172, 198, 237, 275, 298, 299, 347.

101 Ibid., pp. 173, 188, 217, 228.

102 Paine, *Rights of Man*, pp. 64, 66, 67. It is worth noting tangentially that the right to 'consolation in death' is one of the rights that Burke is willing to concede that does exist – *Reflections*, p. 149.

103 Burke, *Reflections*, pp. 194–5, 247.

104 Ibid., p. 272.

105 Burke, *Thoughts on the Cause of the Present Discontents*, p. 122; the emphasis is Burke's. None of this is to suggest that Burke embraces the dead entirely uncritically. In his 'Speech on the plan for economical reform' of 1780 he comments on the absurdity of preserving old establishments as merely a burden when the reason for their preservation has gone. 'This is superstitiously to embalm a carcass not worth an ounce of the gums that are used to preserve it. It is to burn precious oils in the tomb; it is to offer meat and drink to the dead: not so much an honor to the deceased as a disgrace to the survivors.' But such a statement is a rare reversal of his general opinion that the deceased should indeed be honoured. See 'Speech on a plan for the better security of Parliament, and the economical reformation of the civil and other establishments', 11 February 1780, in *The Works of the Right Honourable Edmund Burke*, vol. 2 (London: John C. Nimmo, 1899), p. 305.

106 Burke, *Reflections*, p. 309.

107 Furniss, *Edmund Burke's Aesthetic Ideology*, p. 32.

108 Burke, *Philosophical Enquiry*, pp. 57, 65, emphasis added; also p. 39.

109 Ibid., pp. 40, 59.

110 Ibid., pp. 39–40.

111 Ibid., p. 175.

112 Ibid., p. 43. Likewise, 'Poetry, painting, and other affecting arts . . . are often capable of grafting a delight on wretchedness, misery, and [even] death itself' (p. 44).

113 Ibid., p. 46.

114 G.W. F. Hegel, *Elements of the Philosophy of Right* (1821), trans. H. B. Nisbet (Cambridge: Cambridge University Press, 1991), preface.

115 See Michael O. Hardimon, *Hegel's Social Philosophy: The Project of Reconciliation* (Cambridge: Cambridge University Press, 1994); Steven Sampson, 'From reconciliation to coexistence', *Public Culture*, 15/1 (2003), 181–6.

[116] Burke, *Reflections*, pp. 107, 248.
[117] Beal, *Religion and its Monsters*, p. 10; Richard Kearney, *Strangers, Gods and Monsters: Interpreting Otherness* (London: Routledge, 2003), pp. 34, 120.
[118] Baldick, *In Frankenstein's Shadow*, p. 13.

2 Marx: The Political Economy of the Dead

[1] Karl Marx, *Capital: A Critique of Political Economy*, vol. 1 (1867), trans. Ben Fowkes (Harmondsworth: Penguin, 1976), p. 926.
[2] Stanley Edgar Hyman, *The Tangled Bank: Darwin, Marx, Frazer and Freud as Imaginative Writers* (New York: Atheneum, 1962), p. 145. The citations are from *Capital*, vol. 1, pp. 899 and 915.
[3] Derrida, for example, subsumes the question of the vampire into the spectre. See *Specters of Marx: The State of the Debt, the Work of Mourning, and the New International*, trans. Peggy Kamuf (London: Routledge, 1994), p. 155. One exception to my claim is the excellent discussion of Marx in Chris Baldick, *In Frankenstein's Shadow: Myth, Monstrosity, and Nineteenth-Century Writing* (Oxford: Clarendon Press, 1987), to which I turn on occasion.
[4] Margaret Cohen, *Profane Illumination: Walter Benjamin and the Paris of Surrealist Revolution* (Berkeley: University of California Press, 1993).
[5] Caroline Evans, *Fashion at the Edge* (New Haven: Yale University Press, 2003).
[6] Rob Latham, *Consuming Youth: Vampires, Cyborgs, and the Culture of Consumption* (Chicago: University of Chicago Press, 2002).
[7] Derrida, *Specters*, p. 9.
[8] Karl Marx, *Grundrisse*, trans. Martin Nicolaus (Harmondsworth: Penguin, 1973), p. 162.
[9] Adam Smith, *Inquiry into the Nature and Causes of the Wealth of Nations*, ed. R. H. Campbell, A. S. Skinner and W. B. Todd (Indianapolis: Liberty Fund, 1979), pp. 604–5. On capital as blood see Fred Block, 'Mirrors and metaphors: the United States and its trade rivals', in Alan Wolfe (ed.), *America at Century's End* (Berkeley: University of California Press, 1991).
[10] Terrell Carver, 'Making capital out of vampires', *Times Higher Educational Supplement* (15 June 1984); *The Postmodern Marx* (Manchester: Manchester University Press, 1998), p. 14.
[11] Marx, *Capital*, vol. 1, pp. 342, 367, 416. The quote in the last passage is from Engels's article 'The ten hours bill', 1850.
[12] Marx, *Capital*, vol. 1, pp. 716, 926.
[13] Ibid. pp. 598, 920.
[14] Ibid. pp. 382, 1007.

15   Ibid. p. 348. Engels reiterates the point in *Anti-Dühring: Herr Eugen Dühring's Revolution in Science* (1876–8), trans. Emile Burns (Moscow: Progress Publishers, 1947), p. 191.

16   Christopher Frayling, *Vampyres: Lord Byron to Count Dracula* (London: Faber, 1991), p. 84.

17   Marx, *Grundrisse*, pp. 646, 660.

18   Karl Marx, 'Inaugural address of the international working men's international association' (1864), in Karl Marx and Frederick Engels, *Collected Works*, vol. 20 (London: Lawrence & Wishart, 1985), p. 11.

19   See Francis Wheen, *Karl Marx* (London: Fourth Estate, 1999), p. 283.

20   Marx to Engels, 22 June 1867, in Karl Marx and Frederick Engels, *Collected Works*, vol. 42 (London: Lawrence & Wishart, 1987), p. 383.

21   Karl Marx, *The Class Struggles in France: 1848 to 1850* (1850), in Karl Marx and Frederick Engels, *Collected Works*, vol. 10 (London: Lawrence & Wishart, 1978), p. 94.

22   Karl Marx, *The Civil War in France* (1871), in *The First International and After*, ed. David Fernbach (Harmondsworth: Penguin, 1974), p. 215. The 'First draft' of the text also comments on this 'sucking' tendency (p. 249).

23   Karl Marx, *The Eighteenth Brumaire of Louis Bonaparte* (1852), in Karl Marx and Frederick Engels, *Collected Works*, vol. 11 (London: Lawrence & Wishart, 1979), p. 190.

24   Marx, *Eighteenth Brumaire*, p. 134; *Civil War in France*, p. 219.

25   Frederick Engels, *The Condition of the Working Class in England* (1845) (London: Granada, 1969), p. 264. We have already noted Marx lifting this trope from Engels's essay on the English Ten Hours Bill. As well as the comment cited by Marx above, in that article Engels also describes the system as 'blood-sucking'. See 'The ten hours question', in Marx and Engels, *Collected Works*, vol. 10, pp. 271–2.

26   Karl Marx and Frederick Engels, *The Holy Family, or Critique of Critical Criticism* (1845), in Karl Marx and Frederick Engels, *Collected Works*, vol. 4 (London: Lawrence & Wishart, 1975), p. 203.

27   'Justification of the correspondent from the Mosel', in Karl Marx and Frederick Engels, *Collected Works*, vol. 1 (London: Lawrence & Wishart, 1975), p. 334.

28   Karl Marx, 'The new Prussian constitution' (1849), in Karl Marx and Frederick Engels, *Collected Works*, vol. 9 (London: Lawrence & Wishart, 1977), p. 430.

29   The first is from the *Saturday Review* (18 January 1868), cited in Wheen, *Karl Marx*, p. 311; the second is from the *St Petersburg Journal* (20 April 1872), cited by Marx in his postface to the 2nd edition of *Capital*, p. 99.

30   Robert Paul Wolff, *Moneybags Must be So Lucky: On the Literary Structure of 'Capital'* (Amherst: University of Massachusetts Press, 1988), p. 13.

31   Marshall Berman, *All that is Solid Melts into Air: The Experience of Modernity* (London: Verso, 1983), p. 91; Hyman, *Tangled Bank*, p. 133.

32 These phrases are used in letters to Engels of 31 July and 5 August 1865, written during a period of intensive work on *Capital* – Marx and Engels, *Collected Works*, vol. 42, pp. 173, 174.

33 Wylie Sypher, 'Aesthetic of revolution: the Marxist melodrama', *Kenyon Review*, 10/3 (1948), 431–44, 430.

34 Andrew Smith, 'Reading wealth in Nigeria: occult capitalism and Marx's vampires', *Historical Materialism*, 9 (2001), 39–59, 44, 47.

35 Wheen, *Karl Marx*, p. 305.

36 Wolff, *Moneybags*, pp. 20, 43, 78–9.

37 Chris Baldick and Robert Mighall, 'Gothic criticism', in David Punter (ed.), *A Companion to the Gothic* (Oxford: Blackwell, 2000).

38 Donna J. Haraway, *Modest_Witness@Second_Millenium.FemaleMan©_Meets_OncoMouse™* (London: Routledge, 1997), pp. 214–15.

39 René Girard, *The Scapegoat*, trans. Yvonne Freccero (London: Athlone, 1986), p. 33.

40 For example, Jules Zanger, 'A sympathetic vibration: Dracula and the Jews', *English Literature in Transition 1880–1920*, 34/1 (1991), pp. 33–45; Ken Gelder, *Reading the Vampire* (London: Routledge, 1994), p. 22.

41 Cynthia A. Freeland, *The Naked and the Undead: Evil and the Appeal of Horror* (Boulder, CO: Westview Press, 2000), pp. 123–59.

42 Richard Dyer, 'Children of the night: vampirism as homosexuality, homosexuality as vampirism', in Susannah Radstone (ed.), *Sweet Dreams: Sexuality, Gender and Popular Fiction* (London: Lawrence & Wishart, 1988); Sue-Ellen Case, 'Tracking the vampire', *differences*, 3/2 (1991), 1–20.

43 Bram Dijkstra, *Evil Sisters: The Threat of Female Sexuality and the Cult of Manhood* (New York: Alfred A. Knopf, 1996); Tony Thorne, *Children of the Night: Of Vampires and Vampirism* (London: Victor Gollancz, 1999), pp. 43, 46, 231–3.

44 Judith Halberstam, *Skin Shows: Gothic Horror and the Technology of Monsters* (Durham NC: Duke University Press, 1998), p. 22.

45 Burton Hatlen, 'The return of the repressed/oppressed in Bram Stoker's *Dracula*', in Margaret L. Carter (ed.), *Dracula: The Vampire and the Critics* (Ann Arbor: UMI Research Press, 1988), p. 131.

46 Hatlen, 'Return of the repressed/oppressed', p. 131; Halberstam, *Skin Shows*, p. 88.

47 Halberstam, *Skin Shows*, p. 90.

48 Stephen Arata, *Fictions of Loss in the Victorian Fin de Siècle* (Cambridge: Cambridge University Press, 1996), p. 112.

49 Hatlen, 'Return of the repressed/oppressed', p. 120.

50 Ibid., p. 131.

51 Haraway, *Modest_Witness*, p. 215; David Punter, *The Literature of Terror, Volume 1: The Gothic Tradition* (London: Longman, 1996), pp. 104, 111.

52 Hatlen, 'Return of the repressed/oppressed', p. 122.

53 Baldick and Mighall, 'Gothic criticism', p. 225.
54 Haraway, Modest_Witness, p. 309; Gelder, Reading the Vampire, p. 22.
55 Carver, 'Making capital out of vampires'; Postmodern Marx, pp. 16–18.
56 Frayling, Vampyres, pp. 19, 27; Katharina M. Wilson, 'The history of the word "vampire" ', Journal of the History of Ideas, 46/4 (1985), 577–83; Ernest Jones, On the Nightmare (London: Hogarth Press, 1949), p. 122; Laurence A. Rickels, The Vampire Lectures (Minneapolis: University of Minnesota Press, 1999), p. 15.
57 Frayling, Vampyres, p. 23.
58 M. De Voltaire, A Philosophical Dictionary, vol. 2 (London: Truelove, n.d.), p. 560.
59 Cited in Franco Venturi, Italy and the Enlightenment: Studies in a Comparative Century, trans. Susan Corsi (London: Longman, 1972), pp. 123–4.
60 Jean-Jacques Rousseau, 'Lettre à C. De Beaumont', in Œuvres complètes, vol. 4 (Paris: Gallimard, 1969), p. 987.
61 This is a claim some have made following the work of Taussig. Smith, for example, claims that 'Marx's rhetorical fulcrum . . . relies on an imaginative juxtaposition with images drawn from the pre-capitalist world' ('Reading wealth in Nigeria', p. 45). The argument follows Michael Taussig's work on the occult tropes involved in the culture and resistance of the subaltern worker, in The Devil and Commodity Fetishism in South America (Chapel Hill, NC, 1980). But there is little evidence of the vampire as opposed to, say, the devil, in these tropes; nor is there any evidence that this was Marx's source.
62 Carver, 'Making capital out of vampires'; Postmodern Marx, p. 18.
63 Christopher Frayling and Robert Wokler, 'From the orang-utan to the vampire: towards an anthropology of Rousseau', in R. A. Leigh (ed.), Rousseau after 200 Years: Proceedings of the Cambridge Bicentennial Colloquium (Cambridge: Cambridge University Press, 1982), p. 118; Frayling, Vampyres, p. 34.
64 Voltaire, Philosophical Dictionary, pp. 560–2.
65 See Vincent Carretta, The Snarling Muse: Verbal and Political Satire from Pope to Churchill (Philadelphia: University of Pennsylvania Press, 1983), p. 66.
66 Charles Forman, Some Queries and Observations Upon the Revolution of 1688, and its Consequences etc (London: Olive Payne, 1741), p. 11(a).
67 Cited in Antoine de Baecque, The Body Politic: Corporeal Metaphor in Revolutionary France, 1770–1800, trans. Charlotte Mandell (Stanford, CA: Stanford University Press, 1997), p. 310; also see Marina Warner, No Go the Bogeyman: Scaring, Lulling, and Making Mock (New York: Farrar, Straus & Giroux, 1998), pp. 134–5.
68 Mark Edmundson, Nightmare on Main Street: Angels, Sadomasochism, and the Culture of Gothic (Cambridge, MA: Harvard University Press, 1997), p. 20.

[69] Baldick, *In Frankenstein's Shadow*, p. 148. It should be said that this view contradicts Baldick's earlier (pp. 128–31) and far more compelling argument concerning the vampire as representative of capital.

[70] Franco Moretti, *Signs Taken for Wonders: Essays in the Sociology of Literary Forms* (London: Verso, 1983), pp. 90, 91, 94.

[71] Haraway, *Modest_Witness*, p. 215.

[72] Nicholas Rance, *Wilkie Collins and Other Sensation Novelists* (Rutherford, NJ: Fairleigh Dickinson University Press, 1991), p. 60.

[73] Gelder, *Reading the Vampire*, p. 22.

[74] Halberstam, *Skin Shows*, p. 103. She makes this point despite having just said that Dracula represents a 'monstrous anti-capitalism'.

[75] David J. Skal, *The Monster Show: A Cultural History of Horror* (London: Plexus, 1993), p. 159.

[76] Rance, *Wilkie Collins*, p. 60; Gelder, *Reading the Vampire*, p. 22, emphasis added; Halberstam, *Skin Shows*, p. 103.

[77] That this is so might tell us something important about the 'discipline' of cultural studies and its relation to Marx. The emergence of cultural studies was closely tied with Marxism in Britain. But despite this – or perhaps because of it? – cultural studies has always had a decidedly fractured relationship to Marxism. Stuart Hall once commented that cultural studies can be seen as 'working within shouting distance of Marxism, working on Marxism, working against Marxism, working with it, working to try to develop Marxism' (Hall, 'Cultural studies and its theoretical legacies', in Lawrence Grossberg, Cary Nelson and Paula Treichler (eds), *Cultural Studies* (London: Routledge, 1992), p. 279). However much that may have been true historically, the account of the vampire I have presented here suggests that too many cultural theorists have given up reading Marx in any sustained fashion. Where once this working on/against/within produced work of enormous importance and enviable quality, Marx appears now to be barely read by some cultural theorists. (When I made this point when giving a shorter version of this chapter to the conference *New Myths? Science Fiction, Fantasy and Horror*, at Buckingham Chilterns University College, 3 May 2003, one response from an affronted specialist in cultural studies of the vampire was that I really ought to watch more vampire movies.) This is a shame since, to take one simple metaphor, a more careful reading of Marx may well offer cultural theorists more than they realize. As Marx knew full well, the only thing capital really fears is the 'monster' it has conjured up – the proletariat; everything else, cultural studies included, is a source of profit. Whatever one feels about Marx's use of the vampire that I present here, it cannot be denied that Marx had a far more credible grasp on what he was doing when he invoked the vampire to describe capital. Too many cultural studies, in contrast, have tended to view the vampire through a

distorting lens in which the vampire's otherness and subversiveness (and thus cultural studies' *own* subversiveness) appears everywhere.

But there is also a more substantive political point here. If the power of theory lies in its ability to transform consciousness, to change people and simultaneously spur them to change the world, then the distance between Marx and mainstream cultural studies is even more marked. Marx uses the notion of the vampire to show how capitalism is *literally* founded on the death and constant horror of exploitation. In cultural studies, in contrast, the *metaphorical* is always given more weight than the literal (see Baldick and Mighall, 'Gothic criticism', p. 218). At the conference just mentioned, I pointed out in the discussion that one of the phrases widely used by Goths was 'long live death!', and suggested that it must surely be a concern for cultural studies of the Gothic that this very same slogan was first used by fascists and continues to be adopted by racial nationalists (hence the title and substance of Chapter 3 of this book). The response was that 'they [the Goths] don't mean it'. It is only a metaphor, apparently. Aside from the fact that this does not actually deal with the concern (metaphor or not, it is still a fascist trope), nor that what it is a metaphor of was never exactly explained, it is clear that cultural studies is now so tied to metaphors that it really does not matter if we do not mean what we say. Indeed, maybe it helps if we do not. In this sense, debates about the vampire get reduced to their metaphorically exciting and/or subversive otherness, epitomizing the very procedure which has made cultural studies more or less unable to hold a political position other than one which idealizes a politics of principled uncertainty. Or, worse, one might even suggest that it has in turn *misrecognized* this principled uncertainty and interest in otherness as the only political position worth holding. Either way, politics is thereby collapsed into the cultural; the critique of capital is replaced by textual criticism. Where Marx wanted to spur people into historical action, to liberate the living from the rule of the vampire-capital, mainstream cultural studies collapses history into a universal cod-psychology regarding the liberating power of otherness and tales of its own fantastic, but ultimately fake, subversiveness.

[78] It might just be worth noting that Bram Stoker's *Dracula* was published with that title in June 1897, but as late as 20 May 1897 the correspondence between Stoker and his publishers mentions only his working title for the novel – *The Un-Dead*.

[79] Marx, *Eighteenth Brumaire*, p. 106.

[80] Alexandre Kojève once commented that Marx completely 'neglects the theme of death'. This accusation stems from Kojève's rather obsessive interest in the life and death struggle in Hegel's master–slave dialectic. Because Marx never really discusses this, Kojève assumes that Marx neglects the theme of death. But as this chapter shows, Marx had a very

real interest in *the dead* (though not one that might be particularly
Hegelian). See Alexandre Kojève, 'The idea of death in the philosophy of
Hegel', *Interpretation*, 3/2–3 (1973), 114–57, 156.

[81] Marx, *Capital*, vol. 1, p. 132; Letter to Engels, 24 August 1867, in Marx
and Engels, *Collected Works*, vol. 42, p. 407.

[82] Marx, 'Wage labour and capital', in Karl Marx and Frederick Engels,
Collected Works, vol. 9, p. 215.

[83] Ibid., p. 213.

[84] Marx, *Capital*, vol. 1, p. 342.

[85] Karl Marx, *Economic and Philosophic Manuscripts of 1844*, in Karl Marx
and Frederick Engels, *Collected Works*, vol. 3 (London: Lawrence & Wishart,
1975), pp. 236, 237, 247, 249.

[86] Marx, *Capital*, vol. 1, p. 548.

[87] Ibid., pp. 989–90.

[88] Marx, *Grundrisse*, p. 660.

[89] Marx, *Economic and Philosophic Manuscripts*, p. 278; *Capital*, vol. 1,
pp. 302, 503; *Grundrisse*, p. 831.

[90] Marx, *Capital*, vol. 1, p. 302, emphases added.

[91] Ibid., p. 289. Marx also noted this emergent topsy-turvyness in law. In a
letter to Lasalle from 1862 Marx cites a passage from Vico's 'new science'
in which Vico picks up on the 'poetical' dimension of Roman law: 'ancient
jurisprudence was highly poetical in that it supposed true those facts that
were not so, and refused to admit the truth of facts that were so indeed; in
that it *regarded the living as dead*, and *the dead as living in their
inheritance*'. Marx to Lasalle, 28 April 1862, in Karl Marx and Frederick
Engels, *Collected Works*, vol. 41 (London: Lawrence & Wishart, 1985), p. 357.

[92] Marx, *Grundrisse*, p. 461.

[93] Ibid., p. 364.

[94] Ibid., p. 693.

[95] Ibid., p. 831.

[96] Ibid., p. 454.

[97] Baldick, *In Frankenstein's Shadow*, p. 129; also see Latham, *Consuming
Youth*, pp. 4, 51.

[98] Marx, 'Wage labour and capital', p. 228.

[99] Marx, *Capital*, vol. 1, p. 376.

[100] Ibid., p. 416.

[101] Marx, *Economic and Philosophic Manuscripts*, p. 272.

[102] Ibid., p. 337.

[103] Ibid.

[104] Cited in Karl Marx and Frederick Engels, *The German Ideology* (1845–6),
in Karl Marx and Frederick Engels, *Collected Works*, vol. 5 (London:
Lawrence & Wishart, 1976), p. 104.

[105] Marx, *Economic and Philosophic Manuscripts*, p. 300.

106 Note Ernest Jones: 'It is not without significance that the expression
"Vampirism" was (inaccurately) used to describe the two best-known
cases of necrophilia in the nineteenth century, namely, "Le vampyre de
Paris" for M. Bertrand and "Le Vampyre du Muy" for Ardisson' (*On the
Nightmare*, p. 112).
107 Marx, *Economic and Philosophic Manuscripts*, p. 361.
108 Ibid.
109 Terry Eagleton, *The Ideology of the Aesthetic* (Oxford: Blackwell, 1990),
p. 200.
110 Marx, *Capital*, vol. 1, p. 169; emphasis added. Elsewhere Marx dismisses
Gustav Struve for, amongst other things, suggesting that the four faculties
of the university (theology, law, medicine, philosophy) be replaced with
phrenology, physiognomy, chiromancy and necromancy. See Karl Marx
and Frederick Engels, 'The great men of the exile' (1852), in Marx and
Engels, *Collected Works*, vol. 11, p. 262.
111 Marx, *Capital*, vol. 1, pp. 163–5.
112 Patrick Brantlinger, *Fictions of State: Culture and Credit in Britain,
1694–1994* (Ithaca, NY: Cornell University Press, 1996), p. 148.
113 See here Guy Debord, *Society of the Spectacle* (1967), trans. Black and
Red (Detroit: Black and Red, 1983), para. 2; Slavoj i ek, *For They Know
Not What They Do: Enjoyment as a Political Factor* (London: Verso, 1991),
p. 221.
114 Marx to Ruge, May 1843, in Marx and Engels, *Collected Works*, vol. 3,
p. 134.
115 Marx and Engels, *German Ideology*, p. 137.
116 Karl Marx, 'Wage labour and capital', p. 226.
117 Derrida asks this same question, but his answer is not at all helpful: Marx
'wanted, first of all, it seems, to recall us to the *make-oneself-fear* of that
fear of oneself' (*Specters*, p. 114). Vincent Geoghegan has situated Marx's
comment in the context of his critique of religion. See ' "Let the dead bury
their dead": Marx, Derrida, Bloch', *Contemporary Political Theory*, 1/1
(2002), 5–18. But as I shall aim to show, there is much more to be said
about Marx's comment.
118 Karl Marx, 'Contribution to the critique of Hegel's philosophy of law:
introduction', in Marx and Engels, *Collected Works*, vol. 3, p. 179.
119 Marx, *Capital*, vol. 1, p. 91; *Eighteenth Brumaire*, p. 103; Engels, 'The
future Italian revolution and the socialist party' (1894), in Karl Marx and
Frederick Engels, *Collected Works*, vol. 27 (London: Lawrence & Wishart,
1990), p. 437.
120 Marx, 'Civil war in France', p. 211.
121 Marx, *Eighteenth Brumaire*, pp. 103–4.
122 Ibid., pp. 104–5.
123 Marx, 'Critique of Hegel's philosophy of law: introduction', p. 187.
124 Peter Osborne, 'Remember the future? The Communist manifesto as

historical and cultural form', in *The Socialist Register, 1998* (London: Merlin, 1998), p. 193.

[125] G. A. Cohen, *If You're an Egalitarian, How Come You're So Rich?* (Cambridge, MA: Harvard University Press, 2000), pp. 66–78.

[126] Marx, *Capital*, vol. 1, p. 916. Engels stressed this aspect of vol. 1 of *Capital* in a review of the book he wrote for the *Beobachter* in December 1867: 'he [Marx] endeavours to show that the present-day society, economically considered, is pregnant with another, higher form of society' – Marx and Engels, *Collected Works*, vol. 20, pp. 224–5. It seems that Engels got this idea from a letter from Marx dated from a few days before Engels wrote the review, in which Marx had toyed with the idea of 'hoodwinking' people by writing a review of *Capital* which would stress the point that 'he [i.e. Marx] demonstrates that present society, economically considered, is pregnant with a new, higher form' – Marx to Engels, 7 December 1867, in Marx and Engels, *Collected Works*, vol. 42, p. 494. Engels continued to use the formulation, for example in his discussion of the 'force theory' in *Anti-Dühring*, where he comments (p. 225) that 'force . . . is the midwife of every old society pregnant with a new one'. And note too his comment (p. 129), that 'the feudal Middle Ages also developed in its womb the class which was destined . . . to become the standard-bearer of the modern demand for equality'.

[127] Karl Marx, 'Speech at the anniversary of *The People's Paper*', April 1856, in Karl Marx and Frederick Engels, *Collected Works*, vol. 14 (London: Lawrence & Wishart, 198), p. 655; Marx to Ruge, May 1843, p. 141; Marx, 'Critique of the Gotha programme' (1875), in Karl Marx and Frederick Engels, *Collected Works*, vol. 24 (London: Lawrence & Wishart, 1989), pp. 85, 87; Marx, *Capital*, vol. 1, p. 92; 'Civil war in France', p. 213; Marx, *Capital: A Critique of Political Economy*, vol. 3, trans. David Fernbach (Harmondsworth: Penguin, 1981), p. 966; *Grundrisse*, p. 454.

[128] Karl Marx and Frederick Engels, *Manifesto of the Communist Party* (1848), in Karl Marx and Frederick Engels, *Collected Works*, vol. 6 (London: Lawrence & Wishart, 1976), pp. 507–17.

[129] Marx, 'Critique of Hegel's philosophy of law: introduction', p. 179.

[130] Marx and Engels, *Manifesto of the Communist Party*, p. 499.

[131] Derrida, *Specters*, p. 113.

[132] Marx to Ruge, September 1843, in Marx and Engels, *Collected Works*, vol. 3, p. 144, final emphasis added. As Ernst Bloch puts it in his work on non-contemporaneity: 'the wish for happiness was never painted into an empty and completely new future. A better past was always to be restored too . . . there is no totally new work, least of all of the revolutionary kind; the old work is merely continued more clearly, brought to success' – *Heritage of our Times* (1935), trans. Neville and Stephen Plaice (Cambridge: Polity Press, 1991), pp. 128, 132.

133 This point is made by György Lukács, 'On futurology' (1970), in *The New Hungarian Quarterly*, 13/47 (1972), 100–7, 101.

134 Derrida, *Specters*, p. xix.

135 Christian Lenhardt, 'Anamnestic solidarity: the proletariat and its *manes*', *Telos*, 25 (1975), 133–54.

136 Theodor Adorno and Max Horkheimer, *Dialectic of Enlightenment* (1944), trans. John Cumming (London: Verso, 1979), p. 215.

137 Marx, 'Critique of Hegel's philosophy of law: introduction', p. 186, translation modified.

138 Walter Benjamin, 'On the concept of history' (1940), trans. Harry Zohn, in *Selected Writings, Volume 4: 1938–1940*, ed. Howard Eiland and Michael W. Jennings (Cambridge, MA: Belknap/Harvard, 2003), Thesis II (pp. 389–90).

139 Walter Benjamin, 'N [On the theory of knowledge, theory of progress]', in *The Arcades Project*, trans. Howard Eiland and Kevin McLaughlin (Cambridge, MA: Belknap Press/Harvard, 1999), p. 472. He is citing Julien Benda citing Foustel de Coulanges. He repeats the citation in slightly altered form in Thesis VII.

140 Benjamin, 'On the concept of history', Thesis VII (p. 392).

141 Ibid., Thesis XIV (p. 395).

142 Peter Osborne, 'Small-scale victories, large-scale defeats: Walter Benjamin's politics of time', in Andrew Benjamin and Peter Osborne (eds), *Walter Benjamin's Philosophy: Destruction and Experience* (London: Routledge, 1994), p. 86.

143 Benjamin, 'On the concept of history', Thesis XII (p. 394).

144 Ibid., Thesis VIII (p. 392).

145 Ibid., Thesis VI (p. 391).

146 Ibid., Thesis XVII (p. 396), emphasis added.

147 Ibid., Thesis III (p. 390), translation modified.

148 Ibid., Thesis IX (p. 392).

149 Walter Benjamin, 'Paris, capital of the nineteenth century' (1935), in *Selected Writings, Volume 3: 1935–1938*, trans. Edmund Jephcott, Howard Eiland and others (Cambridge, MA: Belknap/Harvard, 2002), p. 43. On the non-messianic nature of this thesis see Rolf Tiedemann, 'Historical materialism or political messianism? An interpretation of the theses "On the concept of history" ', in Gary Smith (ed.), *Benjamin: Philosophy, Aesthetics, History* (Chicago: University of Chicago Press, 1989).

150 Benjamin, 'On the concept of history', Thesis VIII (p. 392), emphasis added.

151 Walter Benjamin, 'Eduard Fuchs, collector and historian' (1937), in *Selected Writings*, vol. 3, p. 267.

152 Cited by Benjamin, 'N [On the theory of knowledge]', p. 471.

153 Max Horkheimer, 'Thoughts on religion', in *Critical Theory: Selected Essays*, trans. Matthew J. O'Connell and others (New York: Continuum, 1999), p. 130.

154 Horkheimer, 'Materialism and metaphysics', in *Critical Theory*, p. 26.

155 Walter Benjamin, 'Surrealism: the last snapshot of the European intelligentsia'
     (1929), trans. Edmund Jephcott, in *Selected Writings, Volume 2: 1927–1934*,
     ed. Michael W. Jennings, Howard Eiland and Gary Smith (Cambridge
     MA: Belknap/Harvard, 1999), p. 216. Theodor Adorno recognized the link
     between such pessimism and the idea of redemption: 'the only philosophy
     which can be reasonably practised in face of despair is the attempt to
     contemplate all things as they would present themselves from the
     standpoint of redemption' – *Minima Moralia: Reflections from Damaged
     Life* (1951), trans. E. F. N. Jephcott (London: Verso, 1978), p. 247.
156 Walter Benjamin, 'The work of art in the age of its reproducibility' (1936),
     trans. Edmund Jephcott, in *Selected Writings*, vol. 3, p. 108; 'N [On the
     theory of knowledge]', p. 473.
157 Osborne, 'Small-scale victories, large-scale defeats', p. 89.
158 Benjamin, 'Paris', p. 33; 'N [On the theory of knowledge]', p. 459; 'Eduard
     Fuchs', p. 262.
159 Benjamin, 'On the concept of history', Thesis II (p. 390).
160 The Ba'al Shem Tov, cited in Susan Handelman, *Fragments of
     Redemption: Jewish Thought and Literary Theory in Benjamin, Scholem
     and Levinas* (Bloomington: Indiana University Press, 1991), p. 153.
161 Jürgen Habermas, 'Walter Benjamin: consciousness-raising or rescuing
     critique' (1972), in Smith (ed.), *On Walter Benjamin*, pp. 99, 124; Theodor
     Adorno, 'Letter to Benjamin, August 1935', in Theodor W. Adorno and
     Walter Benjamin, *The Complete Correspondence 1928–1940*, trans.
     Nicholas Walker (Cambridge: Polity Press, 1999), p. 106; Axel Honneth,
     'A communicative disclosure of the past: on the relation between anthro-
     pology and philosophy in Walter Benjamin', *New Formations*, 20 (1993),
     83–94.
162 Peter Bürger, *The Decline of Modernism*, trans. Nicholas Walker (Cambridge:
     Polity Press, 1992), p. 22.
163 Benjamin, 'Paris', pp. 33–4.
164 Marx to Ruge, September 1843, p. 144; Benjamin, 'Paris', p. 43. In a short
     fragment entitled 'Agesilaus Santander', written in 1933 on Ibiza in refuge
     from the Nazis, Benjamin comments that the angel looks us in the eye
     and then retreats. Why? 'To draw after himself on that road to the future
     along which he came . . . He wants happiness – that is to say, the conflict in
     which the rapture of the unique, the new, the yet unborn is combined
     with that bliss of experiencing something once more, of possessing once
     again, of having lived' (in *Selected Writings*, vol. 2, p. 715). As Handelman
     comments, 'the only way into the past is via the utopian future, and
     the only way into the future is via the past' – *Fragments of Redemption*,
     p. 170.
165 Walter Benjamin, 'The destructive character' (1931), trans. Edmund
     Jephcott, in *Selected Writings*, vol. 2, p. 542.

166 Benjamin, 'On the concept of history', Theses XV, XVI, XVII (pp. 395–6); 'N [On the theory of knowledge]', pp. 474–5; 'Eduard Fuchs', pp. 262, 268; 'Eduard Fuchs', p. 268.

167 Osborne, 'Small-scale victories, large-scale defeats', p. 91; *The Politics of Time: Modernity and Avant-Garde* (London: Verso, 1995), p. 146.

168 See the entries in the *Oxford English Dictionary*.

169 Adorno and Horkheimer, *Dialectic of Enlightenment*, p. xv.

170 Marx and Engels, 'Great men of the exile', p. 297; Marx, *Class Struggles in France*, p. 58. Also see Marx's letter to Engels of 10 February 1865, in which he talks of an 'evil wind of reconciliation' in Germany – in Marx and Engels, *Collected Works*, vol. 42, p. 85.

171 Benjamin, 'Surrealism', pp. 216–17.

172 See the comments in this regard in Joshua Foa Dienstag, *Dancing in Chains: Narrative and Memory in Political Theory* (Stanford, CA: Stanford University Press, 1997), p. 183. My argument here undermines the idea that reconciliation might contain a utopian dimension recoverable for a Marxist politics. Adorno's later reworking of some of Benjamin's ideas about redemption into the notion of reconciliation is in this sense far less a development of Marxism and far more a slip into conservatism.

3 Fascism: Long Live Death!

1 Adolf Hitler, *Mein Kampf* (1925), trans. Ralph Manheim (Boston: Houghton Mifflin Co., 1943), pp. 40, 43, 44, 50, 324.

2 Ibid., pp. 154, 155, 169.

3 Ibid., pp. 30, 32, 165, 264.

4 Ibid., p. 32.

5 Ernst Nolte, *Three Faces of Fascism: Action Française, Italian Fascism, National Socialism* (1963), trans. Leila Vennewitz (New York: New American Library, 1969), p. 507.

6 Ibid., pp. 508–9.

7 Philippe Lacoue-Labarthe, *Heidegger, Art and Politics: The Fiction of the Political*, trans. Chris Turner (Oxford: Basil Blackwell, 1990), p. 96.

8 This is a point Nolte, *Three Faces of Fascism*, p. 182, makes in relation to Charles Maurras, but it applies equally well if not more so to Hitler.

9 Hitler, *Mein Kampf*, p. 52. Hitler also ponders on whether Marxists are human (p. 41).

10 Schmitt makes the comment in 'Das gute Recht der deutschen Revolution', *Westdeutscher Beobachter* (12 May 1933), cited in Claudia Koonz, *The Nazi Conscience* (Cambridge, MA: Harvard University Press, 2003), p. 2. She also supplies Hitler's use of the phrase.

[11] Hitler in Hermann Rauschning, *Hitler Speaks: A Series of Political Conversations with Adolf Hitler on his Real Aims* (London: Thornton Butterworth, 1939), p. 238.

[12] Saul Friedländer, *Nazi Germany and the Jews: The Years of Persecution, 1933–1939,* vol. 1 (London: Weidenfeld & Nicolson, 1997), p. 100.

[13] Ibid., pp. 100–1.

[14] Stephen Eric Bronner, *A Rumor about the Jews: Reflections on Antisemitism and the Protocols of the Learned Elders of Zion* (New York: St Martin's Press, 2000), pp. 8, 69, 145.

[15] Hitler, *Mein Kampf*, p. 56.

[16] Adolf Hitler, 'Entry for 6th February 1945', in *The Testament of Adolf Hitler: The Hitler–Bormann Documents, February–April 1945,* trans. Colonel R. Stevens, ed. Francois Genoud (London: Icon Books, 1962), p. 47.

[17] Hitler, *Mein Kampf*, p. 307.

[18] Ibid., p. 311.

[19] Ibid., pp. 63–4; 'Speech of 1st August 1923', in *The Speeches of Adolf Hitler, April 1922–August 1939,* vol. 1, trans Norman H. Baynes (London: Oxford University Press, 1942), p. 78.

[20] Hitler, 'Entry for 29th August 1942, evening', in *Hitler's Table Talk, 1941–1944,* trans. Norman Cameron and R. H. Stevens (London: Phoenix Press, 1953), p. 674.

[21] Hitler, *Mein Kampf*, pp. 78, 205, 468; *Hitler's Secret Book* (1928), trans. Salvator Attanasio (New York: Grove Press, 1961), pp. 78, 97, 170; 'Speech of 30th January, 1942', *www.adolfhitler.ws/lib/speeches/text/420130.html* accessed 12 January 2003.

[22] Hitler, 'Entry for 22nd August 1942, evening' in *Hitler's Table Talk*, p. 657.

[23] Hitler, 'Entry for 7th February 1945', in *Testament of Adolf Hitler*, p. 53.

[24] Hitler, Hitler, *Mein Kampf*, p. 386; *Secret Book*, p. 110.

[25] Hitler, Hitler, *Mein Kampf*, pp. 393–5.

[26] Ibid., p. 393.

[27] Ibid., p. 386.

[28] Ibid., p. 394; Friedrich Nietzsche, *Thus Spoke Zarathustra* (1883–5), trans. R. J. Hollingdale (London: Penguin, 1969), p. 75.

[29] Hitler, *Mein Kampf*, p. 374.

[30] Klaus Theweleit, *Male Fantasies, Volume 1: Women, Floods, Bodies, History* (1977), trans. Stephen Conway (Cambridge: Polity Press, 1987), pp. 67, 372.

[31] Ibid., pp. 69–70.

[32] Hitler, *Mein Kampf*, p. 637.

[33] Mark Neocleous, *Fascism* (Milton Keynes: Open University Press, 1997).

[34] Michel Foucault, *The History of Sexuality: An Introduction* (1976), trans. Richard Hurley (Harmondsworth: Penguin, 1979), p. 149.

[35] Benedict Anderson, *Imagined Communities: Reflections on the Origin and Spread of Nationalism,* revised edition (London: Verso, 1991), p. 149.

[36] Judith Halberstam, *Skin Shows: Gothic Horror and the Technology of Monsters* (Durham, NC: Duke University Press, 1998), p. 16; Bram Dijkstra, *Evil Sisters: The Threat of Female Sexuality and the Cult of Manhood* (New York: Alfred A. Knopf, 1996), p. 85.

[37] Bram Stoker, *Dracula* (London: Penguin, 1993), p. 28. References to the novel hereafter appear in parentheses in the text.

[38] John Allen Stevenson, 'A vampire in the mirror: the sexuality of *Dracula*', *PMLA*, 103/2 (1988), 139–49.

[39] Dijkstra, *Evil Sisters*, pp. 91, 264; also see Nina Auerbach, *Our Vampires, ourselves* (Chicago: University of Chicago Press, 1995).

[40] Bram Dijkstra, *Idols of Perversity: Fantasies of Feminine Evil in Fin-de-Siecle Culture* (Oxford: Oxford University Press, 1986), pp. 342, 346, 348.

[41] Halberstam, *Skin Shows*, pp. 91–101; Jules Zanger, 'A sympathetic vibration: Dracula and the Jews', *English Literature in Transition 1880–1920*, 34/1 (1991), 33–44.

[42] Stephen Arata, *Fictions of Loss in the Victorian Fin de Siecle* (Cambridge: Cambridge University Press, 1996), p. 126.

[43] Dijkstra, *Evil Sisters*, p. 230.

[44] Daniel Pick, ' "Terrors of the night": *Dracula* and "degeneration" in the late nineteenth century', *Critical Quarterly*, 30/4 (1988), 71–87, 81. Also see his *Faces of Degeneration: A European Disorder, c.1848–c.1918* (Cambridge: Cambridge University Press, 1989), pp. 55–75.

[45] Michel Foucault, 'The confession of the flesh' (1977), in *Power/Knowledge: Selected Interviews and Other Writings 1972–1977*, ed. Colin Gordon (Brighton: Harvester Press, 1980), p. 223.

[46] J. Gordon Melton, *The Vampire Book: The Encyclopedia of the Undead* (Detroit: Gale Research, 1994), p. 436.

[47] Ken Gelder, *Reading the Vampire* (London: Routledge, 1994), p. 96.

[48] Dijkstra, *Evil Sisters*, p. 427.

[49] Ewers was rather taken by the Nazis during the period of their formation and rise, and was widely respected by them until well into the 1930s. In 1933 Hitler and other leading Nazis decided that a film should be made celebrating the life of Horst Wessel. Given Wessel's importance to the regime (as we shall see later in this chapter), the choice of who should write the film was a crucial and politically sensitive question. The man commissioned by Hitler to write the biography on which a screenplay could be based was the author of one of the best-known vampire novels – Ewers. Figures for Dinter's book are taken from George M. Kren and Rodler F. Morris, 'Race and spirituality: Arthur Dinter's theosophical antisemitism', *Holocaust and Genocide Studies*, 6/3 (1991), 23–52. For the ways in which later films such as *Jew Süss* (1940) came to replicate key aspects of the 'structure of horror' see Linda Schulte-Sasse, *Entertaining the Third Reich: Illusions of Wholeness in Nazi Cinema* (Durham, NC: Duke University Press, 1996), pp. 47–91.

50   Kracauer, *From Caligari to Hitler*, p. 79.
51   Hitler in Rauschning, *Hitler Speaks*, pp. 87–9.
52   Reinhard Koselleck, *Futures Past: On the Semantics of Historical Time*
     (1979), trans. Keith Tribe (Cambridge, MA: MIT Press, 1985), p. 220. See
     for example the extent to which fantastic fears infiltrated the dreams
     reported by Charlotte Beradt in *The Third Reich of Dreams: The
     Nightmares of a Nation 1933–1939* (1966), trans. Adriane Gottwald
     (Wellingborough, Northants: Aquarian Press, 1985).
53   As is well known, from the moment Nazism launched itself on the world it
     relied on what Alfred Rosenberg calls the 'new yet ancient mythos of
     blood'. Clause 4 of the Programme of the German Workers' Party as it
     was transformed into the National Socialist German Workers' Party in
     February 1920 states that 'only those of German blood, whatever their
     creed, may be members of the nation', while key pieces of Nazi legislation
     such as the Nuremberg race laws were created as 'Laws for the Protection
     of German Blood and Honour'. One of the sacred relics of the movement
     was the 'Blood Flag' – the flag carried by the Nazis during their failed coup
     in Munich and supposedly stained with the blood of the martyrs. This
     'religion of blood' is the ideological foundation of the idea that the nation
     is threatened by blood-sucking forces and of the Jews as the 'eternal
     blood-sucker' or 'blood-sucker' with 'poison fangs' (*Mein Kampf*, pp. 54,
     310). Leading Nazis followed the ideological line to the letter. Robert Ley,
     for example, comments on the Jews 'who quite literally sap the blood of
     Gentiles and their children . . . It is only in sucking the blood of other
     peoples that they can preserve their own life', while Nazi propaganda films
     such as *The Crime and Barbarity of the Jews* (1939) and *The Eternal Jew*
     (1939–40) represented the importance of blood to kosher killing as an
     example of Jewish bloodthirstiness. Not only did the symbolic
     significance that the Nazis attached to blood make the bleeding and
     consequent twitching and muscle spasms of the animals seem perverse, a
     form of ritualistic torture or cult of cruelty practised by a coarse and
     unfeeling people, but it also encouraged the view that the blood-sucking
     tendencies would extend to humans too. In other words, the Jews thrived
     only through the vampiric consumption of the blood of humans as well as
     animals. And this biological mysticism was deeply connected to the
     dangerously wandering nature of the Jews. As a nation without a nation
     they lacked any real sense of the importance of blood ties and territory,
     wandering across the globe in a parasitical and imperial fashion and using
     their remarkable mimetic capabilities to assimilate into each nation. As
     Bronner puts it (*A Rumor about the Jews*, p. 46), 'without a homeland,
     wandering the world, the Jew is like the vampire who carries with him his
     coffin partially filled with the soil of his homeland'.
54   Dijkstra, *Evil Sisters*, p. 428.
55   Hitler, *Mein Kampf*, p. 327.

[56] Saul Friedländer, *Reflections of Nazism: An Essay on Kitsch and Death* (1982), trans. Thomas Weyr (Bloomington: Indiana University Press, 1993), p. 75.

[57] Hitler, *Mein Kampf*, pp. 199, 687.

[58] Adolf Hitler, 'Speech at the People's Court, 26 February 1924', in Roger Griffin (ed.), *Fascism* (Oxford: Oxford University Press, 1995), p. 117.

[59] Alfred Rosenberg, *The Myth of the Twentieth Century: An Evaluation of the Spiritual-Intellectual Confrontations of our Age* (1930), trans. Vivian Bird (Newport Beach, CA: Noontide Press, 1982), pp. 460–1.

[60] For the extent to which the Soviet Union failed to participate in this cult of the war dead despite the huge loss of Russian lives between 1914 and 1917, see Catherine Merridale, *Night of Stone: Death and Memory in Twentieth-Century Russia* (New York: Penguin, 2000), pp. 83–5, 93–100.

[61] See Patrizia Dogliani, 'Constructing memory and anti-memory: the monumental representation of fascism and its denial in republican Italy', in R. J. B. Bosworth and Patrizia Dogliani (eds), *Italian Fascism: History, Memory and Representation* (Basingstoke: Macmillan, 1999), pp. 13–15.

[62] Benito Mussolini, 'Trincerocrazia', *Il Popolo d'Italia* (15 December 1917), in *Opera Omnia di Benito Mussolini*, vol. 10 (Florence, 1952), pp. 140–3.

[63] Margherita G. Sarfatti, *The Life of Benito Mussolini* (1925), trans. Frederic Whyte (London: Butterworth, 1926), p. 18.

[64] Cited in Jay W. Baird, *To Die for Germany: Heroes in the Nazi Pantheon* (Bloomington: Indiana University Press, 1990), p. 8.

[65] Gregor Ziemer, *Education for Death: The Making of the Nazi* (London: Constable, 1942), p. 21. During one of the bloody battles of the First World War Hitler's attention was drawn to the high numbers of losses among newly commissioned officers; his only comment was 'but that's what the young men are there for' – cited in Joachim C. Fest, *Hitler* (1973), trans. Richard and Clara Winston (Harmondsworth: Penguin, 1977), p. 25. George Orwell captures the flavour of this in a review of *Mein Kampf* in 1940: 'Whereas Socialism, and even capitalism in a more grudging way, have said to people "I offer you a good time", Hitler has said to them "I offer you struggle, danger and death", and as a result a whole nation flings itself at his feet.' George Orwell, 'Review of *Mein Kampf*', *New English Weekly* (21 March 1940), in *The Collected Essays, Journalism and Letters of George Orwell, Volume 2: My Country Right or Left 1940–1943*, ed. Sonia Orwell and Ian Angus (London: Secker & Warburg, 1968), p. 14.

[66] From the *SS Liederbuch* (Song Book), cited in Heinz Höhne, *The Order of the Death's Head: The Story of Hitler's SS* (1966), trans. Richard Barry (London: Penguin, 2000), p. 2.

[67] Cited in Eugen Weber, 'Romania', in Hans Rogger and Eugen Weber (eds), *The European Right: A Historical Profile* (London: Weidenfeld & Nicolson, 1965), p. 523.

[68] Cited in Ziemer, *Education for Death*, p. 45.

[69] J. P. Stern, *Hitler: The Führer and the People* (London: Fontana, 1975), p. 195.

[70] Rosenberg, *Myth of the Twentieth Century*, p. 463.

[71] Benito Mussolini, *My Autobiography*, trans. Richard Washburn Child (London: Hutchinson, n.d.), p. 121. A law passed by the Nazi regime in February 1934 held that those who had fought for the National Socialist movement were to be granted damages like those who had fought and become victims of the First World War – see Konrad Heiden, *Der Fuehrer*, book 2, trans. Ralph Manheim (London: Victor Gollanz, 1944), p. 575. It is also significant that the official Nazi announcements concerning Hitler's death describe him in this way: 'our Führer Adolf Hitler . . . fell for Germany this afternoon' and 'our Führer, Adolf Hitler, has fallen' – 'Announcement of Hitler's Death, May 1, 1945', *www.adolfhitler.ws/lib/proc/announcment.html*.

[72] Combat 18 in Britain announces its presence in any area it moves into with stickers announcing 'Combat 18 is in the area', accompanied by a black skull symbol.

[73] Cited in Luisa Passerini, *Fascism in Popular Memory: The Cultural Experience of the Turin Working Class* (1984), trans. Robert Lumley and Jude Bloomfield (Cambridge: Cambridge University Press, 1987), p. 104.

[74] Maria-Antonietta Macciocchi, 'Female sexuality in fascist ideology', *Feminist Review*, 1 (1979), 67–82, 71.

[75] I am paraphrasing Adorno on Wagner: 'Behind Wagner's facade of liberty, death and destruction stand waiting in the wings' – Theodor Adorno, *In Search of Wagner* (1952), trans. Rodney Livingstone (London: New Left Books, 1981), p. 14.

[76] The story of Horst Wessel is well-known and does not bear repeating at length here, but the brief details are as follows. Hailing from bourgeois roots in Bielefeld Wessel had, according to the Nazis, learnt the importance of 'sacrifice for the Fatherland' by his father's death during the war. He joined the SA in 1926 and became an agitator and organizer for the NSDAP, especially in the struggle against the KPD in proletarian areas. The record suggests that Wessel was highly regarded by his fellow members as a speaker, leader and composer of party songs. His poem 'Die Fahne hoch' was set to music by Wessel himself and became the anthem of the NSDAP. After his death at the hands of communists in 1930 Wessel quickly became a key figure in the pantheon of dead Nazi heroes. Goebbels in particular saw the death of Wessel as an opportunity to create a Nazi propaganda myth of the highest form. He ennobled Wessel as a warrior hero, an idealistic visionary from a humble background willing to die for the German cause – exemplar of bravery, comradeship, love of country and self-sacrifice for Führer, Volk and Fatherland, Wessel was a

Nazi of the first order. He came to be celebrated in poetry and song, biography and film, party ritual and indoctrination. Town squares and streets were named after him, as were units of the German and Italian armed forces. Hitler named an SA section in his honour, and his grave remained a Nazi shrine until 1945.

77 Hitler, Speech on 22 January 1933, in Max Domarus, *Hitler: Reden und Proklamationen 1932–1945, Volume 1:* (Wiesbaden: R. Löwit, 1973), p. 181. For a slightly different translation see Max Domarus, *Hitler: Speeches and Proclamations, 1932–1945, Volume 1: The Years 1932 to 1934* (London: I. B. Tauris, 1990), p. 220.

78 Cited in Baird, *To Die for Germany*, p. 32.

79 Ibid., p. 33.

80 Discounting the list of names in the 'Dedication', 'Schlageter' is the second proper name of a human being mentioned in *Mein Kampf*. The first is Johannes Palm, who resisted the French troops during the Napoleonic war and was executed by the French in 1806. Both come before any mention of Hitler's parents, despite the focus of the chapter on his upbringing. This has been pointed out and expanded on by Johannes Fritsche, *Historical Destiny and National Socialism in Heidegger's 'Being and Time'* (Berkeley: University of California Press, 1999), p. 249.

81 Heidegger's speech, 'Schlageterfeier der Freiburger Universität' (Freiburg University's celebration of Schlageter) appeared in the *Freiburger Studentenzeitung* on 1 June 1933, p. 1. It was also reported in the *Frankfurter Zeitung* of 27 May and the *Völkischer Beobachter* of 30 May. The text can be found in translation as 'Schlageter', in Richard Wolin (ed.), *The Heidegger Controversy* (Cambridge, MA: MIT Press, 1993), pp. 40–2. References hereafter are to this latter text.

82 Martin Heidegger, *Being and Time* (1927), trans. John Macquarrie and Edward Robinson (Oxford: Basil Blackwell, 1967), p. 240. References are to the marginal pagination which refers back to the original German text.

83 Ibid., pp. 240, 249.

84 Ibid., pp. 258–9.

85 Ibid., pp. 253, 263, 266; emphasis in original.

86 See here Karl Löwith, *Martin Heidegger and European Nihilism*, trans. Gary Steiner, ed. Richard Wolin (New York: Columbia University Press, 1995), pp. 161, 220.

87 Victor Farías, *Heidegger and Nazism* (1987), trans. Paul Burrell and Gabriel R. Ricci (Philadelphia: Temple University Press, 1989), p. 93.

88 Herbert Marcuse, 'The struggle against liberalism in the totalitarian view of the state' (1934), in *Negations*, trans. Jeremy J. Shapiro (London: Allen Lane, 1968), p. 36.

89 Farías, *Heidegger and Nazism*, p. 91.

90 Heidegger, 'Schlageter', p. 41.

91 Martin Heidegger, '25 Jahre nach unserem Abiturium: Klassentreffen in Konstanz am 26/27 Mai 1934', in *Reden un andere Zeugnisse eines Lebensweges, Gesamtausgabe Band 16* (Frankfurt am Main: Vittorio Klostermann, 2000), p. 279.

92 Löwith, *Martin Heidegger and European Nihilism*, p. 220.

93 Theodor Adorno, *The Jargon of Authenticity* (1964), trans. Knut Tarnowski and Frederic Will (London: Routledge & Kegan Paul, 1973), p. 133.

94 A measure of its continued importance can be taken from the websites of the range of groups which go under titles such as 'revolutionary nationalists', 'white nationalists', 'racial nationalists', 'third positionists', and so on. To give just a couple of examples here, see the posted item on the final solution at *http://www.rosenoire.org/essays/final-solution.php.html*, or the essay on the need for mass murder at *http://www.stewarthomesociety.org/gba.html*. For a musical connection see *http://unitedskins.com/interviews/razon.htm*. It is also worth noting that this is a slogan shared by Gothic culture. See, for example, *http://vampires.meetup.com*. It is perhaps also worth noting that the website *longlivedeath.Ff.fm* contains pictures of artwork produced by serial killers.

95 Nationalist Fanzine, *http://dspace.dial.pipex.com/finalconflict/a11-4.html*, accessed 26 February 2003.

96 Cited in Baird, *To Die for Germany*, p. 97.

97 Benito Mussolini, in collaboration with Giovanni Gentile, *Foundations and Doctrine of Fascism* (1932), in Jeffrey T. Schnapp (ed.), *A Primer of Italian Fascism* (Lincoln NE: University of Nebraska Press, 2000), p. 52. Likewise, in his *Autobiography*, p. 124, he comments of a young fascist stabbed to death by communists: 'he declared himself glad and proud to die and that from me he knew how to die'.

98 Klaus Mann's novel *Mephisto* (1936), written while living in exile from Germany, most honestly captures some of these ideas.

99 Cited in Erich Fromm, *The Anatomy of Human Destructiveness* (1973) (Harmondsworth: Penguin, 1977), p. 440.

100 Ibid., p. 441.

101 Elias Canetti, *Crowds and Power* (1960), trans. Carol Stewart (London: Victor Gollanz, 1962), p. 263.

102 Ibid., p. 228.

103 '*Crowds and Power*: conversation with Elias Canetti' (1972), trans. Rodney Livingstone, in Theodor W. Adorno, *Can One Live After Auschwitz? A Philosophical Reader*, ed. Rolf Tiedemann (Stanford, CA: Stanford University Press, 2003), p. 183.

104 Klaus Theweleit, *Male Fantasies, Volume 2: Male Bodies: Psychoanalyzing the White Terror*, trans. Chris Turner and Erica Carter (Cambridge: Polity Press, 1989), p. 19.

105 Sebastian Haffner, *The Meaning of Hitler* (1979), trans. Ewald Osers

(London: Weidenfeld & Nicolson, 1988), pp. 150, 158. Such an inter-pretation is fairly commonplace. For another example see Stern, *Hitler*, p. 209.

[106] Albert Speer, *Inside the Third Reich* (1969), trans. Richard and Clara Winston (London: Sphere, 1971), p. 591.

[107] Michel Foucault, 'Lecture, 17 March 1976', in Michel Foucault, *Society must be Defended: Lectures at the Collège de France, 1975–76*, trans. David Macey (London: Allen Lane, 2003), p. 260.

[108] Gilles Deleuze and Félix Guattari, *A Thousand Plateaus: Capitalism and Schizophrenia* (1980), trans. Brian Massumi (London: Athlone Press, 1987), pp. 230–1.

[109] Foucault, 'Lecture, 17 March 1976', p. 260.

[110] Jean Baudrillard, *Symbolic Exchange and Death* (1976), trans. Iain Hamilton Grant (London: Sage, 1993), p. 186.

[111] 'Entry for 23rd September 1941, evening', and 'Entry for 13th December 1941, midday', in *Hitler's Table Talk*, pp. 38, 144.

[112] Cited in Michael Burleigh, *The Third Reich: A New History* (London: Pan Macmillan, 2000), p. 119.

[113] Hitler, Speech of 8 November 1935, in Max Domarus, *Hitler: Speeches and Proclamations, 1932–1945, Volume 2: The Years 1935 to 1938* (London: I. B. Tauris, 1992), p. 728, emphasis added.

[114] Anacker cited in Baird, *To Die for Germany*, pp. 83–7.

[115] Hitler, *Mein Kampf*, pp. 336, 339, 364, 494, 534.

[116] Ibid., pp. 201, 205, emphasis added.

[117] Heidegger, '25 Jahre nach unserem Abiturium', p. 280.

[118] Hitler, Speech of 8 November 1935, in Domarus, *Hitler*, vol. 2, pp. 726–8.

[119] Hitler, *Mein Kampf*, p. 306.

[120] The idea of resurrection will for many people conjure up the idea of rebirth and would therefore seem to place the argument on the terrain mapped out by Roger Griffin's argument concerning fascism as a palingenetic myth – *The Nature of Fascism* (London: Routledge, 1993). Stemming from the rising again of Christ after death, resurrection does indeed connote rebirth in the literal sense, but is also used to describe the rising again of mankind at the last day; it is the literal process of individual and collective rebirth as part of a new era. But resurrection is also a stronger and more useful category than rebirth. The idea of rebirth in and of itself is hardly fascist – witness Griffin's situating of the revolutions of 1789 and 1989 into the structure of palingenetic myth (p. 34) or, more recently, the plethora of claims and texts on the 'rebirth of Britain' after 1997. The political trope of 'rebirth' can have all sorts of implications – reviving certain institutions, playing a role on the world stage, giving voice to new generations and so on – none of which have any connection with the dead. Thus when it comes to defining fascism in

terms of a palingenetic ultra-nationalism, what is stressed is the rising of the *new* (man, order, nation) out of a period of *decadence*: 'a radically *new* beginning which follows a period of destruction'; a '*new birth*' occurring after a period of perceived decadence' (pp. 33, 36). Because of this, the place of the dead has been relatively unexplored in the literature on the palingenetic myth – relatively unexplored, that is, beyond general points about sacrifice, martyrdom and 'creative destruction'. Indeed, even the fascist stress on sacrifice and martyrdom is presented as 'simply an imaginative version of the cult of the fallen soldier common to all the combatant powers of the First World War', or merely another dimension to the aestheticization of politics 'which no more betokens the presence of a death cult than does the ceremonial honouring of the dead of the two world wars that takes place annually at the Cenotaph in London' – Roger Griffin, 'Shattering crystals: the role of "dream time" in extreme right-wing violence', *Terrorism and Political Violence*, 15/1 (2003), 57–95, 76–7. While my argument picks up on this theme, I am trying to use the idea of *resurrection* rather than simply rebirth to show that there is in fact much more at stake when fascism talks about the dead.

[121] Hitler, 'Entry for 2nd April 1945', in *Testament of Adolf Hitler*, p. 116.

[122] Heinrich Himmler, 'The SS as an anti-Bolshevist fighting organization' (1937), in Griffin (ed.), *Fascism*, pp. 146–8.

[123] The song is from the children's book *Ein Kampft fuers Neue Reich* by Minni Groschtells, which tells the story of German youth fighting communists, cited in Ziemer, *Education for Death*, p. 87.

[124] George L. Mosse, *Fallen Soldiers: Reshaping the Memory of the World Wars* (Oxford: Oxford University Press, 1990), p. 105; George L. Mosse, 'National cemeteries and national revival: the cult of the fallen soldiers in Germany', *Journal of Contemporary History*, 14 (1979), 1–20, 7, 15.

[125] Benito Mussolini, 'Battisti!', 12 July 1917, in *Opera Omnia di Benito Mussolini*, vol. 9 (Florence, 1952), p. 43.

[126] Benito Mussolini, 'All'assemblea quinquennale del regime', 10 March 1929, in *Opera Omnia di Benito Mussolini*, vol. 24 (Florence, 1958), pp. 5–16, p. 16. I have taken the idea of an occult time from Susan Gilman, *Blood Talk: American Race Melodrama and the Culture of the Occult* (Chicago: University of Chicago Press, 2003), p. 201.

[127] Wilhelm Dreysse, 'Die Deutschen von "Langemarck" ', 22 October 1935, cited in Baird, *To Die for Germany*, p. 10. A 1940 quarrel in the *Gräberfürsorge* (Graves Welfare) office of the SS over the markings on the graves of fallen SS men was settled by Himmler's decision that they should be marked with a type of *Lebens-rune* suggestive of immortal life – see Robert A. Pois, *National Socialism and the Religion of Nature* (London: Croom Helm, 1986), p. 64 n. 100.

[128] See the analysis of the collection of biographies of NSDAP members

collated by Abel in James M. Rhodes, *The Hitler Movement: A Modern Millenarian Revolution* (Stanford, CA: Hoover Institution Press, 1980), pp. 61, 69. Also see Theodore Abel, *Why Hitler Came to Power* (1938; Cambridge, MA: Harvard University Press, 1986).

129 Cited in Mosse, 'National cemeteries and national revival', p. 6.

130 Cited in Baird, *To Die for Germany*, p. 8.

131 Cited in Mabel Berezin, *Making the Fascist Self: The Political Culture of Interwar Italy* (Ithaca, NY: Cornell University Press, 1997), p. 202.

132 Emilio Gentile, *The Sacralization of Politics in Fascist Italy* (1993), trans. Keith Botsford (Cambridge, MA: Harvard University Press, 1996), p. 27. The same practice was adopted by the Romanian fascists.

133 Hitler, Speech of 8 November, 1934, in Domarus, *Hitler*, vol. 1, p. 542.

134 Fest, *Hitler*, pp. 761–2.

135 See Jeffrey T. Schnapp, 'Epic demonstrations: fascist modernity and the 1932 exhibition of the fascist revolution', in Richard J. Golsan (ed.), *Fascism, Aesthetics, and Culture* (Hanover: University Press of New England, 1992), p. 30. The importance of resurrection and immortality can also be read throughout fascism's aesthetic self-presentation. For example, the film *Hitler Youth Quex* (1933) tells the story of the youthful exploits of Heini Völker, son of a communist who gradually comes to realize that the future lies with National Socialism not communism. The film ends with the murder of Heini at the hands of a communist. In the montage which follows, Heini's death is replaced by masses of feet marching forward towards the camera as if to march off the screen and into life, conveying the message: the dead carry on marching. Similarly, while Leni Riefenstahl's famous Nazi film *Triumph of Will* posits the idea of a future (modernized, technologically advanced) Germany, it is pitched ultimately at the dead, and the war dead in particular. Laurence Rickels explains: 'the Nazi slogan for the future of a new or true Germany that's been evoked above, around and inside those present . . . is ultimately pitched to the war dead'. And yet we are also told that the war dead are not dead: 'as we get ready to take off for a Germany that's part crypt, part airspace, we still hear the vanishing point that's made in Germany: the lost warriors are undead' – *Nazi Psychoanalysis: Only Psychoanalysis Won the War*, vol. 1 (Minneapolis: University of Minnesota Press, 2002), p. 76. Thus the dead are either not dead but immortal, or they are dead but will be resurrected with the nation. For a discussion of *Hitler Youth Quex* see Linda Schulte-Sasse, *Entertaining the Third Reich: Illusions of Wholeness in Nazi Cinema* (Durham, NC: Duke University Press, 1996), pp. 253–73.

136 Heidegger, *Being and Time*, p. 238.

137 There is now a mass of literature on 'esoteric' Nazism and a substantial portion of it is very poor. Much of the literature stresses the 'magical' and 'mystical' dimension of Nazism, presenting it almost entirely in terms of

the 'religious' and/or quasi-religious practices. As a consequence virtually everything else – slave camps, mass murder, anti-communism, defence of capital, etc. – are more or less written out of the picture. The cult-like obsession with runic symbolism, archaic tropes and occult connections expressed by some authors helps obscure the brutality of the ideology and practice. Nicholas Goodrick-Clarke picks up on this in *Black Sun: Aryan Cults, Esoteric Nazism and the Politics of Identity* (New York: New York University Press, 2002), p. 126, but I think there is far more to be said about it – and some far more political points to be made – than he does or than I have space for here.

[138] Nicholas Goodrick-Clarke, *The Occult Roots of Nazism: Secret Aryan Cults and their Influence on Nazi Ideology* (London: I. B. Tauris, 1992), p. 194.

[139] Walter Benjamin, 'Theories of German fascism' (1930), trans. Jerolf Wikoff, in *Selected Writings, Volume 2: 1927–1934*, ed. Michael W. Jennings, Howard Eiland and Gary Smith (Cambridge, MA: Belknap/Harvard, 1999), p. 321.

[140] Burleigh, *Third Reich*, p. 12.

[141] Paul Gilroy, *Between Camps* (London: Penguin, 2000), pp. 38, 146, notes this constant tendency towards occultism within racial discourse. For a discussion of similar themes within the white separatist movement in America see Mattias Gardell, *Gods of the Blood: The Pagan Revival and White Separatism* (Durham, NC: Duke University Press, 2003).

[142] Frederick Engels, *Dialectics of Nature* (Moscow: Foreign Languages Publishing House, 1954), p. 70.

[143] A good discussion can be found in Reginald H. Phelps, ' "Before Hitler came": Thule society and German Orden', *Journal of Modern History*, 35 (1963), 245–61.

[144] Peter Levenda, *Unholy Alliance: A History of Nazi Involvement with the Occult* (London: Continuum, 2002), pp. 33, 78, 80, 115.

[145] Hitler, *Mein Kampf*, p. 496.

[146] Krohn produced in May 1919 a memorandum 'Is the Swastika suitable as the symbol of the National Socialist Party?' in which he proposed the left-handed swastika (i.e. clockwise in common with those of the theosophists) as the symbol of the DAP. He preferred the sign in this direction on account of its traditional interpretation of fortune and health. The right-handed (i.e. anti-clockwise) swastika, in contrast, symbolized death and decline. Hitler eventually favoured the right-handed (and straight-armed) swastika – see Goodrick-Clarke, *Occult Roots of Nazism*, p. 151. Moreover, fascists understand full well that the flag operates as a means of incorporating the mass of the dead – the *Fahnen* (flag) incorporating the *Ahnen* (ancestors) – Theweleit, *Male Fantasies*, vol. 2, p. 287. For the Gothic dimensions of the swastika see Malcolm Quinn, *The Swastika: Constructing the Symbol* (London: Routledge, 1994), pp. 81–4.

[147] Goodrick-Clarke, *Occult Roots of Nazism*, p. 178; Levenda, *Unholy Alliance*, p. 183.

[148] Goodrick-Clarke, *Occult Roots of Nazism*, pp. 187–8; Levenda, *Unholy Alliance*, pp. 175–6.

[149] Cited by Joachim C. Fest, *The Face of the Third Reich* (1963), trans. Michael Bullock (Harmondsorth: Penguin, 1979), p. 183.

[150] Höhne, *Order of the Death's Head*, p. 154; Hugh Trevor-Roper, *The Last Days of Hitler*, 7th edn (London: Pan Macmillan, 2002), p. 19.

[151] Mussolini, *Autobiography*, p. 119.

[152] And who, for fascism, is the greatest undead of all? None other than the fascist leader himself. The centrality of the leadership principle invariably means that the death of the leader signifies the end of the fascist regime. But the leader is always portrayed as immortal. As such, their death is never quite death. Fascism here plays on the pre-modern trope of the king's two bodies, in which the king was thought to have a body natural, like all other beings, and a body politic, which is utterly devoid of age, infirmity or death. Hence the saying, 'the king is dead, long live the king'. The discourse on the immortality of the leader thus constitutes a fundamental element in the fascist regimes of the twentieth century and, in particular, the more or less absolute power of the Duce or Führer.

It is well known that in terms of his body natural Hitler had no intention of falling 'into the hands of enemies who for the delectation of the hate-riddled masses require a new spectacle' (Hitler, *Last Political Testament*, 29 April 1945, *www.adolfhitler.ws/lib/proc/450429.html*). But by 1945 precisely what should happen to him (that is, his body natural) became a pressing issue. From the moment he thought the nation was facing defeat (i.e. death) he therefore began staging his own. Given the aesthetic and theatrical nature of fascism, it would not have made sense for Hitler to have ended his career with an insipid or bungled *finale*, and in power he had often declared that the only satisfactory death was a spectacular annihilation – to die fabulously. 'In short', he remarked in February 1942, 'if one hadn't a family to bequeath one's house to, the best thing would be to be burnt in it with all its contents – a magnificent funeral pyre!' ('Entry for 17th February 1942, evening', in *Hitler's Table Talk*, p. 316). In other words, he wanted to manage his own death no less than he had managed the death of countless others. The last days of Hitler were thus a carefully produced piece of theatre entirely at one with the aesthetic ambitions of the regime. Hitler's instructions for the disposal of his and Eva Braun's bodies had been explicit: they were to be wrapped in a blanket, carried into the garden by two SS men, and burnt. But what happened to the ashes of the two burned bodies left in the Chancellery Garden has never been discovered. That they were then disposed of in some way remains a possibility, since an open fire will not normally destroy the human body so completely as to leave no traces, and nothing was found in the garden after its capture, despite the initial Soviet claims to the contrary. For this reason rumours quickly emerged that maybe Hitler had survived and spent many a happy day in a bunker in England, on an island in the Baltic, in a Spanish monastery or roving round various parts of South America.

Now, the easy option here is to say that Hitler's survival is a myth constructed by fascists. And, superficially, it can easily seem that fascists (and contemporary racial nationalists) would prefer Hitler to have survived. But this makes neither historical nor political sense. The claim that Hitler survived was made by the Soviet Union during the cold war. Declaring the German assertion that Hitler died in the bunker a 'fresh Fascist trick', the official view from the Kremlin was that 'by spreading statements about Hitler's death, the German Fascists evidently hope to prepare the possibility for Hitler to disappear from the stage and go underground' (*Pravda*, 2 May 1945, cited in Trevor-Roper, *Last Days of Hitler*, p. xlviii). But this says more about Stalinism and the weakness of the Soviet interpretation of fascism than it does about either Hitler's death or fascism itself. This view was peddled either because Stalin believed it or wanted to believe it, or, perhaps more tellingly, because Stalin wanted it to be believed. For what use to fascism is an underground fascist leader, right at the very end of a fascist reign of power? Fascist leaders either have to rule from the stage, in full view of the masses whose will they claim to embody, or they have to be dead – which for them is a form of living anyway. Thus fascists do not have to believe that Hitler 'survived' the bunker to know that he is still alive, for Hitler, as the greatest fascist of all, is of course immortal: the king is dead, long live the king.

Rauschning reports that shortly after the Nazi seizure of power in Germany there were some within the party who believed that 'Hitler dead would be more valuable to the movement than Hitler alive'. The assumption was that Hitler's death would not just be a death. Rather, 'he must disappear into the wilderness; no one must know where; he must be surrounded by mystery and become a legend. A whisper of something portentous to come must run through the masses. The tension must become intolerable.' Dead? Not quite:

> finally Hitler must reappear, metamorphosed, a gigantic figure. He must no longer conduct day-to-day policy; he will be too great for that. As a great law-giver and prophet he must bring from the sacred mountain the new table of commandments. Then, after this last act, he must disappear for ever. But his corpse must not be discovered. For the mass of the faithful he must end in mystery. (*Hitler Speaks*, pp. 161, 279–80)

As Hitler put it, 'my life shall not end in the mere form of death. It will, on the contrary, begin then' (cited in Robert G. L. Waite, *The Psychopathic God: Adolf Hitler* (New York: Basic Books, 1977), p. 20). This idea is pushed to its limit by 'esoteric Hitlerism', which holds that Hitler escaped from the bunker by flying saucer to Antarctica, from where he made it to Venus and/or the 'Black Sun', from where he could more successfully lead the esoteric war. Resurrected, no doubt. Just as Hitler's miraculous powers had once allowed him to present himself, and also to be understood by others, as the *only living unknown soldier* (see, for example, Frederik Böök, *An Eyewitness in Germany* (1933), trans. Elizabeth Sprigge and Claude Napier (London: Lovat Dickson, 1933), pp. 63–75), so his passion for theatrics thus reached its peak with his complete disappearance and transformation into a figure who would remain always somehow undead.

Coda

1   Saul Friedländer, *Nazi Germany and the Jews, Volume 1: The Years of Persecution, 1933–1939* (London: Weidenfeld & Nicolson, 1997), pp. 86–7.
2   James M. Rhodes, *The Hitler Movement: A Modern Millenarian Revolution* (Stanford, CA: Hoover Institution Press, 1980), pp. 58, 68–71; Geoff Eley, 'What produces fascism: preindustrial traditions or a crisis of a capitalist state', *Politics and Society*, 12/1 (1983), 53–82, 81; Michael Burleigh, *The Third Reich: A New History* (London: Pan Macmillan, 2000), pp. 12–13, 258. Also see Joachim C. Fest, *Hitler* (1973), trans. Richard and Clara Winston (Harmondsworth: Penguin, 1977), pp. 101–29, 156; Peter Fritzsche, *Germans into Nazis* (Cambridge, MA: Harvard University Press, 1998), p. 235.
3   'Entry for 13th February 1945', in *The Testament of Adolf Hitler: The Hitler–Bormann Documents, February–April 1945*, trans. Colonel R. Stevens, ed. Francois Genoud (London: Icon Books, 1962), p. 65.
4   Jean-Luc Nancy, *The Inoperative Community*, trans. Peter Connor et al. (Minneapolis: University of Minnesota Press, 1991), pp. 158–9.
5   Rabbi Yitzchok Breitowitz, 'Jewish law articles: the desecration of graves in Eretz Yisrael', *http://www.jlaw.com/Articles/heritage.html*, accessed 18 August 2003.

Index